American Slavery and the American Novel

1852-1977

Edward M. Jackson

Wyndham Hall Press

AMERICAN SLAVERY AND THE AMERICAN NOVEL

1852-1977

Edward M. Jackson

Edward **Merica** Jackson received his Ph.D. in Humanities from Syracuse University and is presently on the faculty of Eastern Connecticut State University.

Library of Congress Catalog Card Number

86-051367

ISBN 0-932269-97-4

TABLE OF CONTENTS

PREFACE

PREFACE

The motivation for this book came because I was interested in the question: Why do Black Americans continue as a group to occupy the lower echelons of American society? Generally, the answer given is that Black Americans are the only ethnic group who endured slavery in the United States.

Early into an investigation of slavery, I concluded that slavery was **not** the explanation for the continued lack of progress of Black Americans. One can argue that slavery in combination with other factors caused Black Americans to be where they are today but it is not slavery alone.

Black Americans, in many ways, overcame slavery. They founded churches, schools, protest organizations, established businesses, created a distinctive interpretation of American culture and even had stable families particularly after slavery.

E. Franklin Frazier has argued that Black Americans' entry into the cities has caused them more problems than any other factor. I would add to his argument that the breakdown of the Black family is a recent phenomenon which began in my generation, those of us who were born during World War Two.

Most of the deterioration of Black life is relatively modern, not more than a generation beginning in the 1960's. Technological, social, cultural and economic changes have contributed to Black Americans' inability to find themselves. Slavery was one cause, not the cause, for Blacks' socio-economic status today.

I continued to research the book because I thought it would be interesting to pursue slavery from a different perspective, that of selected American novels. Slavery in the United States was complex. Although I concluded that slavery is not the single cause of Black Americans' plight, I also concluded that Black Americans still are suffering from some of the legacies of slavery, and like their ancestors, they are still trying to find their place in American society.

CHAPTER ONE

SLAVERY: A POPULAR HISTORY

Slavery in America has its origins in the Renaissance which took place in **fifteenth** century Europe. Many scholars say that the most significant event to take place in human history was the birth of Jesus later proclaimed Christ leading to one of the world's most influential forces, Christianity. If one can accept that thesis, then the migration of Europeans from Europe ranks as the second most important fact of human history.

From the fifteenth century, the Spanish, Portuguese, Dutch, French, and English began to explore Asia and Africa. Breaking away from medievalism in which the Church was central, the emotional or psychological shift from the sacred to secular with the emphasis on **mercantilism**, the Europeans were motivated by economics. They wanted the natural resources of the countries they explored; gold, ivory, fabrics, and foods were their objects. In a word, they wanted **trade**. They not only traded things but they also traded humans.

Once the Europeans got a foothold in Africa and established colonial empires in Africa, they expanded to the Americas. One of the cornerstones of western civilization is the economic system of **capitalism**. Capitalism also has its origins in the Renaissance. With the diminished influence of the Church, lending money was seen as less of a "sin." Under the Medici family, banks began to play an important role in the lives of Europeans. The Western system of capitalism was founded on **credit** and **investment**. One invests in a commodity and that commodity is supposed to create wealth.

Human beings were defined in the European mind set as commodities. They were bought as an investment and sold to make more money. It is not **hyperbolic** to suggest that the rise of the capitalistic system of the western world was based on the **slave trade**.

Once the European nations established their economic empires at the expense of Africa, they later divided the African continent. Africa is still feeling the effects of the European division. We must now turn our attention to how the Africans got to America. Nathan Huggins calls the "exodus" of Africans to the new world "the most traumatizing mass human migration in history" (p. 25). The slave trade did at least two things; it ruptured the African from Africa, and it defined a human being as a thing.

Much has been written about the "midpassage" journey across the Atlantic Ocean. I only need to repeat some of the more salient points. The voyage was dangerous not only for the Africans but also for the European merchants. The voyage was dangerous on all counts. There were storms and heavy winds sometimes battered ships around like small pieces of sticks.

The Africans were loaded, as many as possible, into the holds of the ships. Chained together, there was little room for movement. The Africans wallowed in their own blood, sweat, filth, and disease. Slave ships were death ships for many (p. 53).

One of the myths is that the Africans did not resist the European aggression. Some fought before they were put on the ships. Some fought on the ships, and the Europeans constantly feared that the slaves would mutiny. Others committed suicide.

It is estimated that thirty million Africans were transported from Africa. Nearly half of them died in midpassage. The holocaust of World War Two pales in comparison to fifteen million deaths of Africans. Jewish intellectuals argue that the slave trade took place over a longer period of time, 1619-1803.

The length of time does not diminish the devastating impact that slave trade had on Africa and equally awesome effect it had on the Africans who became American Negroes, Afro-Americans, African-Americans and Black Americans. These various epithets signal the problems Black Americans have had since their sojourn in America.

One of the major problems that Black Americans have had and continue to have is the problem of **identity**. The first Africans who arrived on American soil were not slaves but **indentured servants**. Like Whites, they were brought to the colonies to work for a period of time and become free. It did not work out that way.

2

Virginia, by 1620, had committed itself to a labor system based upon African importation, which led to slavery. Other southern colonies would follow the pattern of Virginia. Slavery did not gain a stronghold in the New England colonies. Part of the resistance to slavery in New England was due to **religion.** The Puritans wanted to find a religious commonwealth, "a city set on a hill," and they devoted their energies to that end. In fact, some of the Puritan leaders, Cotton Mather and Jonathan Edwards, were the first to speak out against slavery. The Anglicans and the Quakers were among the first religious denominations to forbid members of their churches to hold slaves.

Slavery, from the beginning, divided America. The contradictions of slavery in a country professing freedom are apparent. The Founding Fathers were ambiguous at best and hypocritical at worst about it. George Washington, Thomas Jefferson, and James Madison were opposed to slavery in principle,but Washington and Jefferson were slaveholders. Washington and Jefferson freed their slaves upon their deaths but could not muster the moral will to do so during their lives. (One of the studies in this book is that Jefferson sired children by his Black mistress, Sally Hemmings.)

Slavery, in the United States, started haphazardly. It did not become "legal" until 1664, more than a generation after the first Africans landed in Jamestown, Virginia. It lasted more than two hundred years in the United States. Nearly half of Black Americans' experience has been spent in slavery.

Not all Blacks were slaves. Ten percent of the Africans in America have always been free although their freedom was precarious. Another point that needs to be made is that very few Whites owned slaves. Most slaves were owned by one fourth of Whites; the "Gone With the Wind" schema is a myth. Most plantations had less that twenty slaves.

Slavery also was not profitable. Slavery was eroding the economic system of the South in the same way that the segregated public system drained the financial resources of the South. Until Eli Whitney invented the cotton gin, slavery was needed more to serve the psychological needs of white southerners than as an efficient economic system.

By devoting itself to such a system, the South doomed itself to economic dependency on a single crop, primarily cotton. There was tobacco, sugar, and rice but the primary product was cotton. The South did not develop manufacturing like its northern counterpart.

Let me return to a discussion of the slave. To be a slave at best was inhumane and at worst brutal. Slavery, as depicted by the novelists in this study, depended more upon the individual master than it did upon the collective system of slavery. The classic debate about slavery has focused on the Herskovits-Frazier argument. Herskovits maintains along with Lorenzo **Dow Turner** that many of the artifacts of African-isms remained among the slaves. While on the other hand, Frazier maintains that **all** traces of the African heritage were lost. Both positions are correct but Herskovits' theory has become less credible over the years.

The evidence seems to suggest that the African cultural heritage of the slaves was lost due to the process of **acculturation.** Ron Karenga says culture is the totality of a people's thought and practice which occurs in seven basic areas: mythology (sacred and secular), history, social organization, economic organization, political organization, creative production, (arts and sciences), and ethos (collective self-definition and consciousness (p. 207).

If one can accept this as a definition of culture, it is clear that the African lost his culture in America and become "Americanized." The first way this was done was to deprive the African of his **language.** The slaveholders wanted the slaves to work efficiently. To work efficiently, they had to be able to communicate with each other; hence they needed to speak one language. The Africans learned English haphazardly. They retained some of the African words like "goober," "gumbo," "banjo," or "okra," but for the most part, they learned English.

Learning another's language was one process of **acculturation.** What to name themselves was another process of **assimilation.** Some African names such as Juba, Phibbi, Rivah, Kenzia or Sukey were retained until the seventeenth century. As time passed, the Africans began to take the names of the master or some other White person. Booker T. Washington had no last name and he named himself "Washington" after the president.

Most Whites believed that Blacks were incapable of learning the written word; therefore, they kept the slaves illiterate, passing laws against teaching the slaves to read. All Whites did not hold these views and some sympathetic masters taught their slaves to read and write.

4

One of the great achievements of Black Americans is that they became literate by an insatiable thirst for education. Education became like a "god" for the Blacks. After Emancipation, Blacks flocked to schools to learn. It was not uncommon to have a school with a first grade class ranging in ages from five to sixty-five. Later in the classic DuBois-Washington debate the question became: what type of education? That debate is beyond the scope of this study.

Another area where the Africans' culture was taken away was in **religion.** Contrary to popular belief, Black Americans were not "automatically" Christian. Many of the Africans tried to retain the religion of their tribes. One of the differences between American slavery and Latin American slavery was that the Latin slaves fell under the auspices of the Catholic Church. The transition from African religion to Catholicism was an easier one in the Latin American and Caribbean countries. Haiti is a classic example. Religious syncretism became the order of the day. The Haitians combined Catholicism with elements of "vodun."

In America, the situation was different; the United States became predominantly a Protestant nation although so many different ethnic groups came to America and brought so many different religions that a hallmark of America has become **religious tolerance.** Obviously, this has not always been the case. The United States has had periods of anti-Catholicism and anti-Semitism. Most of that is past. The Founding Fathers, in their wisdom, wrote into the Constitution freedom of religion and separation of church and state.

Black Americans, at best, were nominal Christians for at least a century. According to Huggins, the first generation of Africans were, therefore, for the most part, free of systematic Christian religious education (p.72). The slaveholders, at first, rejected Christian instruction for the slaves because they thought it would be incompatible with slavery. Virginia passed a law in 1664 that Christianity and slavery were not inconsistent. When Maryland passed a similar law in 1671, the masters saw religion as another method of **social control** where they could emphasize those doctrines of Christianity which would make the slaves more accepting of their status.

The turning point in the religious history of Black Americans was the Great Awakening of the eighteenth and nineteenth centuries. Where the Anglicans had failed in their attempts to convert the slaves, the Baptists and Methodists succeeded. In their relatively loose and democratic structures, and their unashamed acceptance of spirit and emotionalism, they were the most hospitable to Afro-Americans (p. 73).

Worshipping at first with the Whites and listening to White preachers, the slaves gradually became Christians. Later, Blacks began to find their own churches. Black Americans reinterpreted the Christian religion to suit their needs. They were more interested in the Old Testament than the New Testament but the bottom line is: they became Christian. They adopted the dominant religion of the West and suited it, to use Karenga's word, to their "ethos."

The most serious charge against slavery was that it was an evil system that destroyed the **African family structure.** In every novel included in this study, all of the authors mention the capricious way in which children were separated from their parents. Some slaves lived on different plantations and could only visit their wives and children at the behest of the masters.

Contrary to popular notions, the slaves valued family life. They went to any lengths to protect their families and to maintain family stability. Herbert G. Gutman, in his book THE BLACK FAMILY IN SLAVERY AND FREEDOM 1760-1925, maintains that the breakup of the family during slavery has been vastly overrated. The discussion of the Black family is similar to the discussion of the education of Blacks. The situation is more ambiguous than at first meets the eye. But let me put it like this: slavery did not help the Africans' adjustment to America nor did it strengthen marital bonds or the family.

The story of slavery is one of the most heroic adventures in human history. Ripped from their countries, enslaved, oppressed, brutally treated, the slaves still created what Blasingame calls a "community." They created a family structure where there was none. They were creative in music, giving America the spirituals and gospels and later jazz. They created dances, became expert quilters and influenced the culinary habits of their masters not to mention the sexual mores of the Whites.

When others denied they were humans, the slaves affirmed their own humanity through their desire to be free. One of the mistaken notions about the American slave is that they accepted slavery. Nothing

6

could be further from the truth. They resisted slavery daily (Bauer and Bauer). They broke tools, worked slowly and feigned illness to protest their conditions.

The slaves' rebellion against slavery culminated in 1831 with Nat Turner's rebellion. The revolt of Nat Turner and his men lasted several days in which fifty-seven Whites were killed. It was the most far reaching and influential slave revolt in American history.

It has been said that the Virginians were thinking about ending slavery. The attempts to abolish slavery did reach the state assembly but were voted down. Nat Turner's revolt turned many whites against the Blacks and they became even more repressive. Even with Nat Turner's revolt, some Virginians still wanted to end slavery.

Slavery from its inception in America was wrought with ambiguities. Early, Americans asked the question: how can we be proponents of freedom yet in our midst have slavery? Like many issues in American life, slavery divided America.

Two opposing forces were operative in America until the Emancipation Proclamation. One was the force toward freedom from Great Britain and the other was freedom for the Africans. The colonists linked the problem of slavery to the fight against England. Blacks also petitioned states for their freedom. In the Declaration of Independence, Jefferson lodged the charge against George III that "He has waged war against human nature itself, violating its most sacred rights of life and liberty in the persons of a distant people who never offended him, captivating and carrying them into slavery in another hemisphere, or to incur miserable death in their transportation thither (p. 128). That passage was deleted from the Declaration because of Southern opposition.

At the Constitutional Convention, the issue of slavery was compromised again. Oblique in the Constitution is the idea that government should rest upon property. For the Southern colonies, that meant slaves. The Constitution, in one of its most ignominous compromises, recognized the institution of slavery. By recognizing slavery in both the Declaration of Independence and the Constitution, the burden of slavery now lay on the shoulders of the new nation.

After the American Constitution was ratified, anti-slavery forces grew in number. From the beginning of slavery, small groups of people

7

opposed it; many others supported it. This ambiguity shaped the American attitude. Prominent Americans such as Benjamin Franklin started abolitionist societies. Not only did White Americans work to rid America of slavery but Black Americans also worked to free other enslaved Blacks once they became free. The first great Black leader, Frederick Douglass, was a classic example.

In the nineteenth century, abolitionist forces reached their peak beginning around 1830. Some of the anti-slavery fervor was based on religious beliefs. One of the tenets of Christianity, they claimed, was that all men are created equal in the image of God.

The opposition to the abolitionists was great. They often could not find lecture halls. Often violence visited them. The federal government was indifferent. The abolitionists struggled against great odds.

The South did not stand still while the abolitionists gained strength. They fought back with pamphlets, books, and religion. The pro-slavery argument was divided into four parts. First, they argued that Blacks were inferior in every way to Whites. Second, they found passages in the Bible to justify slavery. Religious denominations split over this interpretation. Third, they argued since the Blacks were inferior they were destined to occupy a subordinate position. Finally, they believed slavery had created a unique way of life in the South based upon the "Southern aristocrat" myth.

With the expansion of the United States, the question of slavery became a national issue. In the 1850's, the struggle over slavery became the issue. The compromise of 1850, the publishing of UNCLE TOM'S CABIN in 1852, the Kansas-Nebraska Act of 1854, the Dred Scott decision in 1857, the raid of John Brown on Harper's Ferry in 1859 all fueled the passion over slavery.

The nomination of a neutral candidate toward abolition but a Republican in 1860 broke the dam for the South. The Southerners identified the election of a Republican, Abraham Lincoln, as an assault on their system. Slavery, according to John Hope Franklin, intensified the reform movements of the nineteenth century. The extent of federal authority was at the heart of the slavery debate and this led to the bloodiest war of the nineteenth century.

The anti-slavery movement had its roots deep in the liberal philosophy of the Revolutionary period, so intersectional strife and the Civil

War itself had their roots in the question of the future of the Negro in the United States (p. 266). The war between the states ended slavery in the United States, but it did not end the debate over the future of Black Americans in the United States, a debate that is renewed with each American generation.

REFERENCES

Bauer, Raymond & Alice, "Day to Day Resistance to Slavery." JOURNAL OF NEGRO HISTORY, October, 1942.

Blasingame, John, THE SLAVE COMMUNITY, 1972.

Brown, William Wells, CLOTEL, OR THE PRESIDENT'S DAUGHTER, New York, MacMillan Company, 1970.

Dubois, W.E.B., THE SOULS OF BLACK FOLKS, New York, Fawcett, 1961.

Franklin, John Hope, FROM SLAVERY TO FREEDOM, second ed., New York, Knopf, 1956.

Frazier, E. Franklin, THE NEGRO FAMILY IN THE UNITED STATES, Chicago, University of Chicago Press, 1939.

Gutman, Herbert G, THE BLACK FAMILY IN SLAVERY AND FREEDOM 1760-1925, New York, Vintage, 1976.

Herskovits, Melville, THE MYTH OF THE NEGRO PAST, Boston, Beacon, 1958.

Huggins, Nathan J., BLACK ODYSSEY, New York, Vintage, 1979.

Karenga, Maulenga, INTRODUCTION TO BLACK STUDIES, Los Angeles, Kawaida, 1982.

Washington, Booker T., UP FROM SLAVERY, New York, Bantam, 1956.

CHAPTER TWO

HARRIET BEECHER STOWE (1811-1896)

Harriet Beecher Stowe was born in Litchfield, Connecticut, on June 14, 1811. She was the daughter of a famous minister, Reverend Lyman Beecher, and the sister of Henry Ward Beecher. Her older sister, Catherine, encouraged her to write. She moved to Cincinatti at eighteen. She married Calvin Ellis Stowe, a professor in the Lane Theological Seminary, and spent eighteen years living across the river from a slave state.

UNCLE TOM'S CABIN, written after the Stowes had moved to Maine, brought its author immediate world-wide fame. This melodramatic history of the relations of a group of Southern White families and their slaves is one of the most influential works in American literature.

If ADVENTURES OF HUCKLEBERRY FINN is a racist novel, then what is UNCLE TOM'S CABIN?

UNCLE TOM'S CABIN is one of those books described by Leslie Fielder as a great book but a bad novel or a bad book but a great novel. It is like the discussion of the ending of ADVENTURES OF HUCKLE-BERRY FINN. Critics and scholars ask how could a novel so great end so poorly. One could ask the same question about UNCLE TOM'S CABIN. How can a novel so sentimental, so melodramatic, and so unrealistic have such power over the reader?

First, one has to put the book into historical perspective. Like many novels of the nineteenth century, it is romantic and melodramatic. One of the most famous scenes in the novel is Eliza's escape with babe in arms across the Ohio River filled with masses of ice. She jumps on a fragment of ice, leaps to another and still another cake of ice, stumbling, leaping, slipping, and springing upwards again (p. 62)! She makes it to the other side of the river where she is helped by a Quaker.

Obviously, Eliza's escape strains the imagination. If the reader is concerned only with verisimilitude, the reader will miss the power of Stowe's perspective. First, like a Spielberg movie, the scene tugs at the reader's heart because the reader is on the side of Eliza. We want her to escape. She immediately becomes the heroine and her pursuer, Haley, becomes the villain.

Second, the scene is archetypal, illustrating the limits to which a mother will go to protect her child. Finally (and perhaps more to the heart of Stowe's thesis), it portrays the central evil of slavery---the separation of child from mother. Even though the scene is unrealistic, it grabs the reader with its power.

The greatness of the novel is not in its consistent realism but in its characterization. We remember the characters; we feel with them. The reader feels the pathos of Eliza, the anger of George Harris, the goodness of Eva, the sad ambiguity of Mrs. Shelby toward slavery and the quiet dignity of Tom. In Simon Legree, Mrs. Stowe created one of the great villains in American literature.

Like many novels of the nineteenth century, UNCLE TOM'S CABIN is both realistic and melodramatic. The realism is in the unrelenting depiction of slavery as a moral evil. When Mrs. Stowe takes us inside the slave cabin and describes the cabin in detail, that is realism.

One of the problems an author like James Baldwin has with the novel is the portrayal of Tom. Uncle Tom, trustworthy and sexless, needed only to drop the title "Uncle" to become violent, crafty, and sullen, a menace to any white woman who passed by (Baldwin, NOTES OF A NATIVE SON, p. 21). Tom is a one dimensional character according to Baldwin.

One must hasten to argue, in Mrs. Stowe's defense, that she invests Tom with **dignity.** The question that comes to mind is: is Tom realistic? Were Blacks as passive and accepting of their fate as Tom? There is evidence that some Blacks were loyal to their masters and some even refused to leave them when set free by the Emancipation Proclamation. But Blacks like Tom were an aberration. Most Blacks fled slavery like a plague when Union armies invaded the South.

One must also keep in mind that UNCLE TOM'S CABIN is a thesis novel. Through the character of Tom, Mrs. Stowe is presenting the thesis that Christianity and slavery are antithetical. When we meet Tom, he is being taught to read the Bible by "Mas'r" George. Tom not only wants to be "better" but he also wants to be a "better" Christian. Tom was a sort of patriarch in religious matters in the neighborhood (pp. 31-32). Mrs. Stowe also sets Tom up as a figure of absolute goodness. He is the most beloved slave on the plantation. Everyone acknowledges that Tom is steady, capable, and honest. But Mr. Shelby has to sell him (along with Harry, Eliza's baby) to pay off a debt. This incident sets in motion the drama of the novel. When Tom finds out that he has been sold, he says, "I'm in the Lord's hand, nothin' can go on furder than he lets it; and thar's one thing I can thank him for. It's me that's sold and going down, and not you nur the children. Here you're safe; what comes will come only on me; and the Lord, he'll help me, I know he will" (p. 97).

Tom's Christianity is a type of **fatalism**. He accepts everything which happens as the will of God. In the midst of the worst thing that happens, separation from his family, Tom sees some "good" in it and does not despair. This is a classic statement of Christianity: hope triumphs over despair and good triumphs over evil.

Stowe's depiction of Tom being sold and separated from his family is realistic. This attitude toward being sold seems unrealistic. What slave would be thanking God for being sold? The novel continues to combine realism with melodrama.

I have already spoken of the unlikely coincidence connected with Tom. When he is being transferred down the river, he meets Little Eva; they immediately become friends, and when she falls in the river, he saves her. He is bought by her father, St. Clare, a good master. Interestingly enough, he is not a Christian.

Coincidences upon coincidences pile up in the novel. St. Clare is portrayed as a "good master." He lets Tom have "free" reign over the plantation and Tom becomes Little Eva's best friend. It is like the relationship of Shirley Temple and "Bojangles" Robinson in the movies.

I have asked the question: if ADVENTURES OF HUCKLEBERRY FINN is a racist novel, then what is UNCLE TOM'S CABIN? There is a belief shared by many that mulattoes or light-skinned Blacks are more intelligent than dark-skinned Blacks. UNCLE TOM'S CABIN shares the idea. All of the intelligent Blacks in the novel, Eliza and George Harris, are mulattoes. All of the illiterate or ignorant Blacks are dark skinned.

The most famous example is Topsy. When Ophelia first sees her, she asks, "Augustine, what in the world have you brought that thing here for?" (p. 239). Miss Ophelia defines a human as a "thing." This is part of the American racist psyche. Blacks are not seen as human. This ambiguity is also captured by the American Constitution when the "Founding Fathers" defined slaves as three-fifths of a person.

The task St. Clare has given Ophelia is to educate Topsy. Topsy is totally ignorant. When asked who made her, her famous reply is, "I spect I grow'd. Don't think nobody never made me" (p. 243).

Mrs. Stowe, quite naturally, contrasts Topsy with Eva. There stood the two children, representatives of two extremes of society. The fair, high-bred child, with her golden head, her deep eyes, her spiritual, noble brow, and prince-like movements; and her black, keen, subtle, cringing, yet acute, neighbor. They stood as the representatives of their race. The Saxon born of ages of cultivation, command, education, physical and moral eminence; the Afric, born of ages of oppression, submission, ignorance, toil, and vice (p. 247)!

Although Mrs. Stowe is trying to be sympathetic, if this is not a racist statement, I don't know what is. It is obvious that Mrs. Stowe is not a historian. She is not aware of the bloody wars of English history over religion and government and wars with the French.

We know today that Africa produced some of the great thinkers. St. Augustine was an African. We also know that until Europeans came to Africa, Africans had "high" culture based on the extended family and they made significant contributions to culture.

Mrs. Stowe asks, "what is to be done with Topsy?" (p. 247). We are still asking this question today. What are we to do with the Topsies that we confront? To Mrs. Stowe's credit, Topsy is not hopeless. She does learn and she does change. It is through Little Eva's tenderness that Topsy becomes more "civilized." The Christian Mrs. Stowe makes the point that Christianity can change anyone, including Topsy.

I argue that this is a racist perspective, that it is an accepted axiom that Christianity is the "superior" religion and that Anglo-Saxon culture is superior to any other culture.

One of the most sentimental scenes in the novel is the death of Little Eva. When Eva is dying, the servants are brought to her bedside and she says, "I am going to leave you. In a few more weeks, you will see me no more" (p. 289). Eva's talk is interrupted by bursts of groans, sobs, and lamentations (p. 289). This is not unrealistic in the sense that many slaves did cry at the death of a beloved master or mistress. The sentimentalism is the excess of emotions shown by the slaves. Even Topsy cries at Little Eva's plight.

Tom is most devoted of all to Miss Eva, sleeping outside her window, ready to rouse at every call (p. 294). On the day of Eva's death, Tom goes to get the doctor. St. Clare turns away in agony and with tears streaming down his dark cheeks, looks up for help where he had always been used to look (p. 296). Eva dies and says "O, love-joy-peace!" (p. 297).

Tom is more concerned about his master's plight than he is about himself. Tom tries to convert St. Clare. "I's willing to lay down my life, this blessed day to see Mas'r a Christian" (p. 303). To a twentieth century Black, Tom's behavior is even more offensive when St. Clare says one day "well, Tom, I'm going to make a free man of you; so have your trunk packed, and get ready to set out for Kentucky" (p. 306). Tom refuses to leave until Master's troubles are over. "And when will my trouble be over?" asked St. Clare. "When Mas'r St. Clare's a Christian," said Tom (p. 307). St. Clare never becomes a Christian because he is killed trying to break up a bar room brawl.

Upon St. Clare's death, Marie becomes distraught and mean. She decides to sell some of the slaves, including Tom, although St. Clare has promised Tom his freedom. When Tom hears that he is going to be sold again, he says, "The Lord's will be done" (p. 323). Tom never wavers in his faith. In Tom, Stowe combines characteristics of Job and Christ.

Simon Legree, one of the most infamous characters in American literature, is introduced late in the novel. Much like Huck's father, he is a supporting character but leaves an indelible memory on the reader. He is described as a short, broad, muscular man of gigantic strength. He seized Tom by the jaw and pulled open his mouth to inspect his teeth; made him strip up his sleeve to show his muscle, turned him round, and made him jump and spring to show his paces (pp. 334-335).

15

Thus, Tom is introduced to his new master. Simon Legree treats Tom just the opposite of St. Clare. Stowe again shows how slavery depends upon the caprice of the owner. In Simon Legree, she shows the worst side of slavery, the brutal master who has no regard for the dignity or humanity of the slaves.

Further evidence of Legree's cruelty is when he takes Tom's clothes and sells them. He also takes Tom's hymnal away. "...I remember. Now mind yourself...I'm your church! You understand--you've got to be as I say" (p. 339).

Tom hides his Bible from Legree and one can only wonder what would have happened to Tom if he could not have had his Bible. In the early part of the novel, the reader was taken inside of Tom's cabin; he had "decent" quarters where he stayed with his wife and son. Now he is brought to one of the most dilapidated plantations ever; he also discovers that he has to live communal-style surrounded by other slaves with no privacy, privacy Tom needed after work to read his Bible.

Tom resumes his old role as the spiritual leader of the plantation. Tom's goodness is seen by the other slaves and he soon gains their respect. The relationship of Tom to Simon Legree is reminiscent of the relationship of John Claggart to Billy Budd. Legree does not like Tom. Like Claggart and Billy Budd, they are opposites. They are good and evil contrasted.

Tom, from an external perspective, is passive but from another perspective, Tom is a rebel. Tom rebels when he tries to help his fellow slaves. He shows kindness to a young mulatto girl, brought into the fields to pick cotton. He tries to transfer some of his cotton to her bag. When she resists, "O, you mustn't! You dunno what they'll do to ye!", Tom says "I can bar it! Better n' you" (p. 354). This is one way in which Tom rebels.

Another way he rebels is through his passive resistance to Simon Legree. Legree wants Tom to become an overseer because of his qualities of leadership. When Tom refuses to beat a slave girl, Legree strikes him with a cowhide and pelts Tom with a shower of blows (p. 357).

Tom's refusal raises Legree's ire. He cannot accept one of his slaves' refusal to obey him. "An't I yer master? Didn't I pay down twelve hundred dollars, cash, for all there is inside yer cussed black shell? An't yer mine, now body and soul?" he said, giving Tom a violent kick with his heavy boot, "Tell me!" "No! No! No! My soul an't yours, Mas'r! You haven't bought it, ye can't buy it! It's been bought and paid for, by one that is able to keep it; no matter, no matter, you can't harm me!" (p. 358).

This is a classic confrontation between good and evil. Legree lives by the laws of nature; Tom, however, lives by a higher law, the law of God. This dichotomy is Augustinian. St. Augustine paralleled the laws of God and the laws of man in THE CITY OF GOD. Though a semi-illiterate slave, Tom clings to and understands that his soul does not belong to an earthly creature like Legree but only God can claim his soul.

In contrast to Tom is the character of Cassy. She defies Legree but she doubts that God exists. When she goes to minister to Tom and tells him of the brutality of Legree, she says, "you tell me...that there is a God, a God that looks down and sees all these things. Maybe it's so...I used to love God and prayer" (p. 368).

Cassy is more concerned with this world. Because of this concern, she plots to escape from Legree's plantation. Along with another slave woman, Emmeline, she decides to run away. On the night they decide to escape, Cassy goes to Tom and implores him to go with them. Tom refuses to go with her; he says "the Lord's given me a work among these poor souls, and I'll stay with 'em and bear my cross with 'em till the end" (p. 400).

Tom sees his responsibility to the other slaves. He does not deter Cassy. When she has made up her mind to leave, Tom says "the Lord help ye!" (p. 400).

Tom never gives up his faith. The two slaves succeed in their escapes and hide in Legree's garnet. Legree, filled with outrage, feels that Tom knows where they have gone. When Legree, Sambo, and Quimbo come to get Tom, he knows that day of his death has come. "Into thy hands I commend my spirit! Thou hast redeemed me, oh Lord God of truth" (p. 414). Stowe continues to compare Tom's ordeal to that of Christ. When Tom is killed by Simon Legree, he prays for Legree's soul, a true Christian martyr. Even Sambo and Quimbo are touched by Tom's faith.

Stowe spares us the details of Legree's brutality toward Tom causing his death. The reader can see the brutality of slavery through Tom's death. She has made her point. Then she lapses back into a series of coincidences.

Young George Shelby has been on a journey to retrieve Tom. Through haphazard luck, he arrives at Legree's plantation and finds Tom near death. Then through sentimental dialogue, Tom praises the Lord for seeing Mas'r George for the last time. He tells George not to tell Chloe, his wife, how he found him. When George speaks of revenge against Legree, Tom says "Don't feel so! He an't done me no real harm--only opened the gate of the kingdom for me; that's all" (p. 421). In Tom's death, he conquered the evil of Simon Legree.

George buries Tom on the plantation. Simon Legree deteriorates into a drunkard, drinking imprudently and recklessly (p. 426). Through another coincidence, Cassy met George on the boat to freedom. Cassy is, at first, apprehensive about George thinking that he might figure out that she escaped from Legree. Later she finds out that George is a good man.

On the boat is a Madame de Thoux who we find out is George Harris' sister. Then Cassy discovers that Eliza is her long-lost daughter. Upon finding out this information, she faints, a nineteenth century romantic convention. All of them are rejoined together in Canada as free persons. They go to France and finally settle in Liberia. George Shelby returns home and frees all of his slaves.

So what do we make of UNCLE TOM'S CABIN? UNCLE TOM'S CABIN, a runaway best seller upon publication, was a controversial book from the beginning. According to the legend, when Abraham Lincoln met Mrs. Stowe, he is supposed to have said, "So this is the lady who wrote the book that started the war." The book had supporters and detractors from its inception. Most people could not believe that slavery was so cruel. Others said such characters could not exist. Some did not believe that Mrs. Stowe was the author because she was a woman.

In her concluding remarks, Mrs. Stowe (like Mark Twain) says most of what she wrote was true, based on her observations or that of friends. Mrs. Stowe says, in effect, that whether or not what she wrote is true is not the point, but that Christians remain silent on the issue of slavery and, in fact, through their silence, support slavery.

It is not just a southern problem but also a northern problem. She writes: Both North and South have been guilty before God, and the Christian church has a heavy account to answer (p. 451). Though thoroughly dissimilar, these words could have been written by James Baldwin if one substitutes the word "slavery."

I think the power of the book is similar to that of ADVENTURES OF HUCKLEBERRY FINN. The book's themes are at the heart and center of the central conflict in the American democracy, the conflict between slavery and freedom. The book is powerful because it deals with the problem of race in American society. We, as a nation, still ask the question, "what shall we do with Topsy?".

REFERENCES

Baldwin, James, NOTES OF A NATIVE SON, New York, Bantam, 1972

Gossett, Thomas F., UNCLE TOM'S CABIN AND AMERICAN CUL-TURE, Southern Methodist Press, Dallas, 1985.

Melville, Herman, BILLY BUDD, New York, Signet, 1961.

Stowe, Harriet Beecher, UNCLE TOM'S CABIN, New York, Perennial Classics, 1965.

Twain, Mark, ADVENTURES OF HUCKLEBERRY FINN, ed. Sculley, Bradley, New York, Norton, 1977.

CHAPTER THREE

CLOTEL, OR THE PRESIDENT'S DAUGHTER

WILLIAM WELLS BROWN (1816?-1884)

The birth of Black fiction came in the 1850's with the publication of three novels, one by a runaway slave and two by free Blacks. One of the first novels written by a Black person was in 1853 by William Wells Brown and was titled CLOTEL, OR THE PRESIDENT'S DAUGHTER. Brown was born near Lexington, Kentucky, the son of a White father and a mulatto slave mother who was rumored to be the daughter of Daniel Boone. As a young man, Brown, who was known only as William until his escape from slavery, moved with his master to Missouri where he was assigned the task of house servant and where he was later rented to the St. Louis publisher, Elijah P. Lovejoy. In his autobiography, THE NARRATIVE OF WILLIAM WELLS BROWN (1847), Brown recounts his experiences before and after his escape from slavery.

Brown lectured in England on behalf of the society for several years and was in London when he wrote and published CLOTEL in 1853. He later wrote three plays, the first written by a Black American; Milinda, or The Beautiful Quadroon (1855); Experience, or How to Give a Northern Man Backbone (1856); and The Escape, or A Leap for Freedom (1858). None of the plays is extant, nor, as far as can be learned, were any ever produced. Newspaper accounts of Brown's lecturing activities suggest that Brown read excerpts from the plays to his abolitionist audiences.

CLOTEL, OR THE PRESIDENT'S DAUGHTER is a novel filled with stereotypes. It has the slave auction, the mulatto theme, the hypocritical Christian who justifies slavery and the foolhardy slaves who try to be "white." As a novel of propaganda, the author succeeds, but the novelist fails as a novelist. He is presenting a point of view which he belabors relentlessly. The people in the novel are stock characters. Except for rare instances, they do not "live and breathe."

Like Stowe, Brown portrays the plight of the mulatto as "tragic" while depicting the darker skinned Blacks like Sam as buffoons. There are some poignant incidents in the novel like the two slaves who run away and engage in "ride and tie" (p. 132). Two slaves pretend one of them is a runaway. One of them rides the horse while the other is tied to a rope to deceive any Whites who come along. When they reach free territory, they give up their guise and pursue freedom.

Brown had all of the stock scenes of an anti-slavery tract. He shows the Blacks running away and hunted by the most vicious of dogs. While he describes this action, he will put excerpts of newspapers which have no relationship to the present narrative.

Despite the structural flaws of the novel, Brown presents a wicked view of slavery. He shows the vagaries and vicissitudes of slavery. A slave might have one master one day and another master another day. There is the example of a woman born in Germany but thought a mulatto and reduced to slavery.

The dominant theme of the novel is hypocrisy. Hypocrisy is in three forms, sexual hypocrisy, religious hypocrisy and political hypocrisy. The sexual hypocrisy is the White man's lust for the Black female. This lust produced the mulatto class. For Brown, this is the best evidence of the degraded and immoral condition of the relation of master and slave in the United States (p. 36). Often "negro balls" were held but they were White men with their mulatto and quadroon mistresses.

The sexual tension depicted by Brown occurred when a white man brought his quadroon mistress to his house. In Clotel's case, the mistress ordered her to cut off her hair. One of Brown's theses is that the lust for Black females went to the uppermost levels of the society touching some of America's greatest figures including Thomas Jefferson.

Brown does not spare any wrath for religious hypocrites. Frederick Douglass said that the worst thing that could befall a slave was to have a "Christian" master.

The criticism of Christianity in the book is centered around the character of Rev. John Peck. The Reverent Peck is an apologist for slavery. He sees no contradiction in holding slaves and being a Christian minister. Indeed, he believes that it is his duty to teach the slaves the gospel.

In contrast, Georgiana (his daughter), questions slavery. When she makes a long speech to her father (in the convoluted style in which Brown writes) about the rights of the slaves and implies that slavery is wrong, her father replies, "Georgiana, my dear, you are an abolitionist; your talk is fanaticism" (p. 68).

Rev. Peck does have preachers come to speak to his slaves. The type of religion preached to them is: serve your masters faithfully, because of their goodness to you (p. 72). One of the classic questions is: how did the slaves respond to the messages to remain subservient? Most scholars agree that they adopted the "gospel" to their own purposes and many of them rejected the Whites' interpretation. For example, Aunt Dafney, a slave on the Peck plantation, says, "Dey all de time telling dat de Lord made us for work for dem, and I don't believe a word of it" (p. 75).

Uncle Simon, who fancies himself a preacher, replies, "thars more in de Bible den dat..." (p. 75). This type of response gave rise to two different interpretations of the gospel. Later, when Independent Black Churches were found, Blacks would use religion not only as a technique of survival but also as an instrument to gain their freedomm.

The sexual and political hypocrises of the novel are wound up in the character Clotel. The book begins with the sale of Currer and her two daughters, Clotel and Althesa. Currer is alleged to have been the mistress of Thomas Jefferson and the two daughters of Currer are his children.

Currer brought up her daughters to "attract" the company of White men; therefore, she had them go to "negro balls" of which I have written. But her plans are thwarted when she and her daughters are sold. The mother and Althesa are sold to Dick Walker and Clotel is sold to Horatio Green who takes her as a mistress.

Slavery, in many instances, was as cruel or tolerable as the master. Dick Walker was an irresponsible master. He gambles and gets in debt. To pay off his debt, he has to sell Currer without her daughter. Brown makes the observation that selling human beings was very casual.

Brown skips around so much in the book that it is confusing. He returns to the story of Clotel who has borne a child, Mary, for Horatio Green.

He keeps Clotel as a mistress, but because of laws at that time and possibly his own inclination, he does not marry her. Instead, he marries Gertrude because of the necessity of circumstances (p. 82).

Some months after they were married, Clotel and her daughter were walking along the road when Gertrude exclaimed, "Do look at that beautiful child" (p. 83). When Horatio sees them, his face grows pale. Soon after she learned the truth and wept silently. Therefore, an archetypal paradigm is set; the White female tolerates the former liason of her White husband but is vengeful in her heart.

To forget about his trouble, Horatio Green turns to the bottle. To salvage his marriage, Clotel is sold and her daughter, Mary, is brought into the Green household by Mrs. Green out of vindictiveness. Mrs. Green compels Mary to do the dirtiest and meanest work that she can find. Horatio Green sees his own daughter mistreated but does nothing about it, an archetypal pattern.

Clotel is sold to Mr. James French, a merchant. His wife sees her as a threat and has her to cut her hair. Clotel goes on a hunger strike and she is sold again. When Clotel settles into her new status, she is befriended by William, a slave mechanic. Together they plot to escape.

Brown employs the technique, popular in nineteenth century sentimental novels, of the **disguise motif.** Dressed as a man, Clotel escapes into Cincinatti, Ohio. However, she returns South to find her daughter.

When Clotel returned to Richmond, the Whites were up in arms because of Nat Turner's insurrection. The Blacks were being arrested, beaten and killed. Because of this aroused state, the Whites were on lookout for strangers. While searching for fugitives, the police arrest Clotel after they discover that she is s woman.

She is placed in prison and is later to be transported by boat to New Orleans. When they are taking her from the jail, she runs, throws herself over a bridge and commits suicide. Thus died Clotel, the daughter of Thomas Jefferson, a president of the United States; a man distinguished as the author of the Declaration of American Independence, and one of the first statesmen of that country. They have tears to shed over Greece and Poland; they have an abundance of sympathy for "poor Ireland," they can furnish a ship of war to convey the Hungarian refugees (p. 177-178), but for Clotel there is not even

24

the simplest dignity of a burial. She is thrown into a hole after being washed ashore. Her only crime in life is that she was born a slave. It was not her color that doomed her but her social status.

Althesa is bought by James Crawford, a person emotionally opposed to slavery. He purchased Althesa to work in his household rather than to keep her as a slave. When he brings her home, Henry Morton, a young physician, falls in love with her and in an unusual act, he marries her. They have two daughters, Ellen and Jane.

In one of the most convoluted of propagandistic novels, Brown has the Mortons to die leaving their daughters to his brother. When the brother comes to New Orleans to claim them, he finds out that they are slaves. When he offers to buy them, the creditors "claim" they could get more for them on the open market.

Ellen commits suicide when she is sold to a man who wants her for a concubine, and her sister Jane dies of a broken heart when her lover is killed trying to help her escape. Much has been written of the plight of the mulatto women in the novel and the fate they suffered. All of them come to a tragic end, at least in this book.

In an incredible plot, Brown has one of the slaves who engaged in the rebellion be the slave of Horatio Green who has fallen in love with his daughter Mary. George joined the rebel forces and is to be hanged. In a series of improbable events, Mary goes to visit George and they exchange clothes. As George was of small stature, and both were White, there was no difficulty in his passing without detection. She usually left the cell weeping, with handkerchief in hand, and sometimes at her face, so he had only to adopt this mode and his escape was safe.

George wants to make good his promise (p. 184) to get Mary out of slavery. He employed a missionary to find out about Mary's status. Because Mary had assisted in his escape, she had been sold again. Incredibly, George leaves the United States, establishes himself in England, and a few paragraphs later, he is wealthy.

Then, through an incredible incident, George observed a lady in black with a black veil over her face. The woman faints twice in George's presence and he is puzzled. Then he is invited to dinner by a J. Devenant. The woman who had fainted twice in his presence was Mary, his old love. Mary relates what happened to her after George's escape.

25

Indeed, she was sold but Devenant buys her freedom and marries her. Brown says it is the country's shame that George and Mary can receive protection from any of the governments of Europe, but they can not return to their native land without becoming slaves.

Brown anticipates his reader's question: Are the various incidents and scenes related founded in truth (p. 201)? He answers that the stories related in the narrative are true and are a composite of stories that he had experienced or had heard about.

REFERENCES

Farrison, W. Edward. "The Origin of Brown's Clotel," PHYLON, XV (1954), 327-347.

Farrison, W. Edward. "Phylon Profile XVI, William Wells Brown," PHYLON IX, (1948), 13-25.

Farrison, W. Edward. WILLIAM WELLS BROWN, University of Chicago: Chicago, 1969.

Lewis, Richard O. "Literary Conventions in the Novels of William Wells Brown," CLA Volume XXIX, Number 2, Dec., 1985.

.

CHAPTER FOUR

BLACK READERS AND MISINTERPRETATIONS OF THE CHARACTER OF JIM IN ADVENTURES OF HUCKLEBERRY FINN

MARK TWAIN (1835-1910)

Samuel Langhorne Clemens, the third of five children, was born on November 30, 1835, in the village of Florida, Missouri, and grew up in the larger river town of Hannibal, that mixture of ideal and nightmare in and around which his two most famous characters, Tom Sawyer and Huck Finn, live out their adventure-filled summer. Sam's father, an ambitious and respected but unsuccessful country lawyer and storekeeper, died when Sam was twelve, and from that time on Sam worked to support himself and the rest of the family. Perhaps as more than one critic has remarked, the shortness of his boyhood made him value it the more.

ADVENTURES OF HUCKLEBERRY FINN took Twain eight years to write. He began in 1876 and completed it in 1883. The fact that he devoted seven months to subsequent revision suggests that Twain was aware of the novel's sometimes discordant tones and illogical shifts in narrative intention. Any real or imagined flaws in the novel, however, have not bothered most readers. Huck Finn has enjoyed extraordinary popularity since its publication nearly 100 years ago. Its unpretentious, colloquial, yet poetic style, its wide-ranging humor, its embodiment of the enduring and universally shared dream of perfect innocence and freedom, its recording of a vanished way of life in the pre-Civil War days, has endeared it to many. Mississippi Valley has moved millions of people of all ages and conditions and all over the world. It is one of those rare works that reveals to us the discrepancy between appearance and reality without leading us to despair of ourselves or others.

In a casual telephone call to my sister, she remarked to me that her fourteen year old daughter was upset because she had read HUCKLE-BERRY FINN for the first time. It seemed that she was upset for two reasons. First, she did not like the copious use of the word "nigger" throughout the story and second, she did not like the way Jim "talked."

A Black school board member of a Long Island school district, at the behest of Black parents, brought it to the attention of the school board that HUCKLEBERRY FINN should be banned as required reading for the two reasons which my niece pointed out. In addition, he added that Jim is not a "typical" Black person and does not represent "Black interests" today.

The first example belongs to the category of an "emotional interpretation" of a work of literature; the second raises the question of censorship and its problems in a democratic society. Censorship is one of the most complex problems in a free society and it is one of those issues which people on both the left and the right advocate at certain times. The question of censorship is not the issue pursued in this discussion. The issue which I would like to explore is how Black readers read ADVENTURES OF HUCKLEBERRY FINN. First, the "language" or the way Jim "talks" strikes a raw nerve. Second, the word "nigger" disturbs them; finally, many take issue with the characterization of Jim.

Let us begin with the language. In the explanatory introduction to the novel, Mark Twain goes to no small length to say that a "number of dialects are used, to wit: the Missouri Negro dialect."[1] He adds that they "have not been done in a haphazard fashion or by guesswork, but painstakingly, and with the trustworthy guidance and support of personal familiarity with these...forms of speech."[2]

The language of HUCKLEBERRY FINN has always been a source of debate. It is not only Jim who speaks in a certain way which Blacks may consider "offensive," but HUCKLEBERRY FINN has been removed from many library shelves because Huck "fractures" the English language. The point is that Twain was trying to reproduce the common language of mid-nineteenth century America that qualified the book as "realistic." It is not meant as an offense to any ethnic group but an attempt to portray the language of the people at that time.

The use of the word "nigger" is not an indication of Twain's intolerance but the word was used in pre-Civil War America as synonymous with slaves. For the most part, the word is derogatory, but the treatment of Black Americans at the time was particularly derogatory. As one of my professors at Syracuse University said, "everybody in the nineteenth century was a racist."

The use of the word "nigger is complex. For Blacks, the word can be degrading when used by Whites. When Blacks use it with each other, it can mean different things depending upon the tone, the situation, and the relationship between the speakers. Before his accident, Richard Pryor used the word profusely in his act, and one of his albums, entitled "This Nigger is Crazy," won a Grammy as the best comedy album of the year. In his filmed concert, "Richard Pryor on the Sunset Strip," he vowed never to use the word again because of his experience in Africa. While in Africa, he saw no "niggers" there and concluded that there must not be any. However, Blacks still use the word in a complex matrix, but this belongs to the category of "ethnic prerogative." Blacks use it when talking to each other but they do not tolerate it when other groups use it. To return to Mark Twain, he was using the word as a reflection of his time.

More importantly is the interpretation or mis-interpretation of Jim by Black Americans. The obvious mistake that Blacks make is that they fail to see the complexities of Jim.[3] Ralph Ellison asserts that "the Negro is made uncomfortable" by the appearance of Jim in the novel. He claims that Jim belongs to the minstrel tradition. His reading of the novel suggests that Huck is always a man and Jim is always a boy. He adds that the relationship of Jim and Huck "comes across as that of a boy for another boy rather than as the friendship of an adult for a junior."[4]

Even as astute an artist as Ellison mis-reads the complexity of the relationship between Huck and Jim. It is no wonder that a fourteen year old girl studying at a parochial school would misinterpret it. Daniel G. Hoffman says, "insufficient notice has been taken of the ways in which Jim, as well as Huck, grows to maturity and assumes a man's full obligation."[5] The evolution of Jim's character and the changing nature of his relationship to Huck should be apparent to the cursory reader but evidently it is not since the character of Jim makes the Black reader "uncomfortable."

Now let me examine the complexities of the character of Jim and how his relationship to Huck changes. There are several indications of Jim's complexities in the novel. First of all, Jim is superstitious; however, his superstitions are shared by the culture of the day. Namely, he believes in ghosts, the devil and witches. Jim gains a certain notoriety because of his ability to tell stories about witches. Like Huck, he lies but the lies are meant to entertain and not to hurt anyone. In telling the stories, Huck says about Jim, "every time he told it he spread it more and more..."[6] Because of his skill as a story teller, other Blacks would come from miles around to hear Jim's stories. Huck adds that "Jim was most ruined, for a servant, because he got so stuck up on account of having seen the devil and been rode by witches."[7] Therefore, another quality of Jim is that he is **proud.**

Huck also looks up to Jim. When he has problems, he turns to Jim. Many critics[8] have suggested that Jim is Huck's spiritual father." At first, Huck has troubles with his father and he asks Jim what should he do. Jim does not give a satisfactory answer but the point to see is that Huck sees Jim as a **friend** and **father-confessor.**

Jim and Huck share a common desire and that is to be **free.** Jim wants to be free from slavery; Huck wants to be free from bourgeois encumbrances. If the quest for freedom is atypical of Blacks, then we have seriously misread contemporary history.

Jim and Huck are both **pariahs.** They become outcasts because they are seeking freedom. They are "thrown" together and form a community. It is not a "legal" or an "easy" community. As a runaway slave, Jim has violated the law. As a White, Huck also has broken the law because he aids and abets a runaway slave. He is obligated to turn Jim in to the proper authorities. It is this uneasy and illegal relationship which evolves as they flee down the river.

There is no question that Jim matures as a character and that Huck's attitude toward him changes. There are several instances of Huck's immaturity and Jim's maturity in the novel. The first occurs during the storm. Jim exclaims, "Well, you wouldn't a ben here, 'f it hadn't ben for Jim. You'd a ben down deah in de woods widout any dinner, en gittn' mos' drownded, too, dat you would, honey. Chickens knows when it's gwyne to rain, enso do de birds, chile."[9] Jim takes care of Huck; Jim stands watch in Huck's place and builds the wigwam on the raft. Jim is a compassionate figure to be admired and is not one to be denigrated.

Another episode occurs when the House of Death floats by. It is Jim who goes aboard and discovers a dead body. He says, "Come in, Huck, but doan' look at his face--it's too gashly."[10] Jim comprehends the horror of the dead man's murder and he protects Huck from cruel knowledge that the dead man is Huck's father. Jim begins to assume the role of Huck's metaphorical father.

In this incident, Jim acts as the adult and Huck acts as the boy. Huck is more concerned about the booty, "an old tin lantern, and a butcher knife without a handle, and bran new Barlow knife..."[11] while Jim is aware of the mysteries of death and the cruelties of men toward one another.

Huck's psychological attitude toward Jim, as Ellison points out, is that of a White toward a Black which inculcates superiority. However, Huck's attitude toward Jim is a continual movement toward equality and a recognition of Jim's humanity. This is indicated by a series of episodes. The first happens when Huck puts a snake in Jim's blanket. The snake bites Jim on the heel. It is Jim who directs Huck with his folk wisdom, maintains his poise and tells Huck exactly what to do. Huck feels ashamed because of what he did to Jim so he throws the snakes out. He says, "I warn't going to let Jim find out it was all my fault, not if I could help it."[12] In this passage, Huck's growing respect for Jim's feelings emerge.

When Jim gets better, Huck goes ashore dressed as a girl. While on shore, he discovers that there is a reward out for Jim. His disguise is found out, but more importantly, he runs back to the raft to warn Jim, "Git up and hump yourself, Jim! There ain't a minute to lose. They're after us."[13] It is significant that Huck says "us." At this point, he identifies with Jim's plight.

As Huck begins to understand that his fate and Jim's are inseparable, they are separated by a fog. Huck sees this as an opportunity to play another trick on Jim. Huck claims that he had been on the raft all along. Jim says he must "terpret" it.[14] When Jim looks at the leaves, the rubbish on the raft, and the smashed oars, he realizes that Huck has played a trick on him.

> What do dey stan' for? I's gwyne to tell you. When I got all wore out wid work, en wid de callin' for your, en went to sleep, my heart was mos' broke bekase you wuz los', en I didn't k'yer no mo' what become er me en de raf'. En when I wake up en fine you back agin', all safe en soun', de tears come en I could a got down on my knees en kiss yo' foot I's so thankful. En all you wuz thinkin' 'bout wuz how you could make a fool uv ole Jim wid a lie. Dat truck is dah is trash; en trash is what people is dat puts dirt on de head er dey fren's en makes 'em ashames.[15]

32

According to Hoffman, this is the turning point of the novel in terms of Huck's relationship to Jim. Jim makes an eloquent statement about the nature of friendship. He is a figure of dignity and maturity in contrast to Huck's puerile antics. It is here that Huck recognizes Jim's humanity. He discovers that his ties to Jim are greater than his ties to society. The society asserts that Whites are superior to Blacks. When Huck sees that his actions have made Jim depressed, Huck acts.

> It was fifteen minutes before I could work myself up to go and humble myself to a nigger, but I done it, and I warn't ever sorry for it afterwards, neither. I didn't do him no more mean tricks, and I wouldn't done that one if I's a knowed it would make him feel that way.[16]

This is no static relationship. The emphasis should not be on the word "nigger" but on Huck's changing attitude toward Jim. The contrast should be noted between Jim's adult behavior and the childishness of Huck. The key moral crisis of the novel occurs in chapter sixteen when Jim and Huck arrive in Cairo, Illinois, a free state. Jim begins to talk avidly of freedom. Huck exclaims, "it made me all over trembly and feverish"[17] to hear Jim exult about his freedom. One could argue that Jim is a **militant.** He says,

> I's a free man, en I couldn't ever be free ef it hadn't ben for Huck; Huck done it. Jim won't ever forget you, Huck; you's the bes' fren' Jim's ever had; en you's de only fren' ole Jim's got now...de on'y white genlman dat ever kep' his promis to ole Jim.[18]

These are not the words of a Black man which should inspire shame. Jim keeps life in perspective. He knows that the most important thing in life is freedom and he also knows that he cannot trust White people.

The dictates of society claim that Huck should turn Jim in. Huck makes up his mind that he is going to turn Jim in the first chance he gets. Shortly afterwards, Huck meets some slave hunters who present him with his opportunity to turn Jim over to the "proper authorities." They ask him, "Any men on it?" (the raft). Huck replies, "Only one sir." They ask, "Is your man white or black?" Huck struggles with his conscience and says, "He's white."[19] Not only does he say Jim is White but he also calls him "pap." Continuing to lie, he claims that Jim has smallpox. With this information, the slave hunters leave. Huck has lied to save Jim. The moral ambiguity of Huck's dilemma cannot be overstated. He disobeys an unjust law to observe a higher one. This is a philosophical question which has been debated from Socrates to today. However, Huck has not reconciled his "feelings" about equality. His crisis will be resolved in chapter thirty-one.

From chapter sixteen onward, Jim becomes a minor character. Huck and Jim are separated; Twain introduces the Duke and the Dauphin as characters and the Grangeford-Shepherdson feud as an episode. There has been considerable discussion about the ending of HUCKLE-BERRY FINN. I need to say a few more things about the ending to conclude my discussion and then give an overview on how Blacks misinterpret the character of Jim.

Critics such as Leo Marx have pointed out the lapse of imagination by Mark Twain in the ending of the novel. Other critics have also pointed out that the ending of the novel still has flashes of brilliance. The key villain is Tom Sawyer. Putting the ending in perspective, Judith Tetterley has seen the denouement as an attack upon Tom Sawyer and romanticism.

These points aside, there are three incidents which corroborate Huck's maturity. The first is the final resolution of Huck's moral dilemma. He decides to write a note to Miss Watson telling her that Jim is on the Phelps' farm. He adds, "I felt good and all washed clean of sin for the first time I had ever felt so in my life..."[20] But he has a change of heart; he starts thinking about the voyage down the river and all that he and Jim had been through. He looked at the note and studied it and then said, "All right, then, I'll go to hell" and tore it up.[21]

When Huck sees Jim as a person and not as a slave, he reiterates the "code of the river" which he and Jim have established. Part of the code suggests that one treats a friend in a certain way; in this particular instance, one frees one's friend from slavery.

The second episode indicative of the maturation of Huck is his response when he sees the Duke and the Dauphin carried out of town on a rail; they were tarred and feathered. Huck responds, "It was a dreadful thing to see. Human beings can be awful cruel to one another."[22]

This is a boy who is full of compassion. As Henry Nash Smith points out, he has "a sound heart and a deformed conscience."

The final incident is when he discovers that Tom Sawyer has been deceiving them all along, that Jim is free, that Miss Watson is dead, and that Aunt Sally wants to adopt him. Huck thinks it over and says, "...I reckon I got to light out for the Territory ahead of the rest, because Aunt Sally she's going to adopt me and sivilize me and I can't stand it. I been there before."[23] Twain returns to the dominant theme of the novel, the quest for freedom.

As far as Jim is concerned, his status and characterization do change when the Duke and the Dauphin come on the raft. Jim does, in fact, become a minstrel figure, painted and dressed as an Arab. He is subjected to burlesque, an object of Tom Sawyer's slapstick and romantic lunacy. A preposterous rescue is concocted by Tom although Jim is already free. Despite the fact that Huck has matured, based upon his experiences on the river, he comes under the sway of Tom Sawyer. In the final episodes, both Huck and Jim are divested of their dignity.

Despite this, Hoffman argues that regardless of the debasement of Jim in these final episodes, he still remains a figure of dignity. Hoffman says that Jim has achieved "spiritual freedom." It is testimony to his moral stature and fortitude that he understands freedom apart from the antics of Tom Sawyer. Hoffman concludes that Jim's dignity is manifested by the fact that he helps Tom when he becomes sick. Before an angry mob, he does not point out Huck lest he involve him in this unpleasant turn of affairs. "Jim's loyalty is so great that he is willing to sacrifice his freedom for his young friend's sake. His selflessness is truly noble, a far cry from the chuckleheadedness of the slave"[24] in the first part of the novel.

If one looks at the character of Jim, there is no question that the character grows throughout the novel, that Huck's attitude toward him changes, and that Jim is a figure of dignity and uncommon resolve. Jim should not be expected to speak with a New England accent; he is, like most Blacks at that time, illiterate. If one turns to a more recent work of literature, ROOTS, by Alex Haley, we find that the Black characters in that novel speak in much the same way that Jim does. The obvious difference is that one author is White, writing in the nineteenth century, and the other author is Black, writing in the twentieth century. Ethnic prerogative prevails.

The use of the word "nigger" was a common term during the nineteenth century. During the sixties, Black Americans' disdain for the word caused them to change their racial name to "Black" because "Negro" sounded too much like "nigger." One of the mistakes that Blacks make in interpreting the character of Jim is that they apply twentieth century "sensibilities" to nineteenth century realities.

Finally, to denigrate Jim is a gross misinterpretation of his character. Nat Hentoff, in a television debate on the first amendment, paid the highest compliment to Jim when he said, "Jim is the only adult in the novel who has any integrity, the only adult who does not exploit others for personal gain." The fact that ADVENTURES OF HUCKLE-BERRY FINN still causes such strong emotions says something about the power of the novel and something about unresolved problems of race relations in American society.

FOOTNOTES

1. Mark Twain, ADVENTURES OF HUCKLEBERRY FINN, ed. Sculley Bradley, et. al. (New York: Norton, 1977) p. 2.

2. Twain, p. 2.

3. Ralph Ellison, "Change the Joke and Slip the Yoke," in ADVENTURES OF HUCKLEBERRY FINN, ed. Sculley Bradley (New York: Norton, 1977) p. 421.

4. Ellison, p. 422.

5. Daniel G. Hoffman, "Black Magic--and White--in Huckleberry," in ADVENTURES OF HUCKLEBERRY FINN, ed. Sculley Bradley, et. al. (New York: Norton, 1977) p. 426.

6. Twain, p. 11.

7. Twain, p. 11.

8. Sculley Bradley, ed. ADVENTURES OF HUCKLEBERRY FINN, Hoffman, Marx, et. al.

9. Twain, p. 44.

10. Twain, pp. 44-45.

11. Twain, p. 45.

12. Twain, p. 46.

13. Twain, p. 54.

14. Twain, p. 71.

15. Twain, p. 72.

16. Twain, p. 72.

17. Twain, p. 73.

18. Twain, p. 74.

19. Twain, pp. 74-75.

20. Twain, p. 169.

21. Twain, p. 169.

22. Twain, p. 182.

23. Twain, p. 229.

24. Hoffman, p. 431.

REFERENCES

Ellison, Ralph, "Change the Joke and Slip the Yoke," in ADVENTURES OF HUCKLEBERRY FINN, ed. Sculley Bradley. New York: Norton, 1977.

Fetterly, Judith, "Disenchantment: Tom Sawyer in HUCKLEBERRY FINN," in ADVENTURES OF HUCKLEBERRY FINN, ed. Sculley Bradley. New York: Norton, 1977.

Haley, Alex. ROOTS. New York: Dell, 1977.

Hoffman, Daniel G., "Black Magic--and White--in HUCKLEBERRY FINN," in ADVENTURES OF HUCKLEBERRY FINN, Sculley Bradley. New York: Norton, 1977.

Pryor, Richard, "This Nigger is Crazy."

Pryor, Richard, "Richard Pryor: Live on Sunset Strip"

Smith, Henry Nash. "A Sound Heart and a Deformed Conscience," in ADVENTURES OF HUCKLEBERRY FINN, ed. Sculley Bradley. New York: Norton, 1977.

Twain, Mark. ADVENTURES OF HUCKLEBERRY FINN. ed. Sculley Bradley. New York: Norton, 1977.

CHAPTER FIVE

JUBILEE: A STUDY IN CONTRASTS

MARGARET WALKER (1915-)

Margaret Walker was born in Birmingham, Alabama, in 1915. She attended the public schools of the south and went to the midwest to complete her higher education. Her novel, JUBILEE, is one of the great historical novels in American literature.

The story of her great-grandmother, Vyry, was the subject of her doctoral dissertation at the University of Iowa. The novel won the Houghton Mifflin Literary Award in 1966.

Margaret Walker spent most of her academic career teaching at Black colleges, specifically, Jackson State University in Jackson, Mississippi. She has also published several poems over the years. The most widely known is "For My People" which is included in her volume of poetry FOR MY PEOPLE.

JUBILEE has been described as an epic novel. It is the story of the author's maternal great-grandmother, Vyry. It is a "personal" novel based on an account of Margaret Walker's relatives. Like many of the novels previously discussed, the mulatto theme is paramount. Vyry, Margaret Walker's great-grandmother, like many mulattoes, had a father who rejected her. That is the central event of her life. The consequences of her father's rejection is that she had to spend her life as a slave rather than as a free person.

Walker's novel, unlike Stowe's, is **historical.** It ranges from ante-bellum slavery to reconstruction. It begins with the death of Sis Hetta, John Dutton's Black mistress who has borne fifteen children. He had banished Vyry to another plantation. Hetta's last wish is to see her daughter. Dutton reluctantly agrees and Vyry sees her mother for the last time.

Because her father rejects her, Vyry, in effect, grows up an orphan but she does have mother surrogates on the plantation. Mammy Sukey, the cook, serves as her first mother surrogate and teaches her to cook; later, she becomes the cook of the "big house."

There are several incidents in the novel which illustrate the tragic consequences of slavery. The first one has been alluded to; Vyry's rejection by her father. The second is the separation of Vyry from her mother. This separation of child from mother and the debilitating effects on the Black family has been described as the worst effect of slavery.

A point which needs to be made is that the cruelty of slavery was more often than not dependent upon the caprices of the master. In Vyry's case, her master was her father. He was no less cruel because of that.

In this novel. the tension between the mulatto offspring of the master and the master's wife is depicted. Salina, the master's wife, is seen as a sexless woman who got no enjoyment out of sex. She saw sex only for the sake of procreation (p. 9). She refrained from having sex with Joh Dutton. Therefore, he turned to Hetta, his Black mistress. This is the archetypal pattern of the double standard of White male sexual attitudes. He places the White female on a pedestal, creating a madonna figure. At the same time, he debases the Black female, making her his concubine.

When Vyry is taken to the "big house" to work, she comes into contact with Salina who hates her. This hatred is illustrated when Vyry forgets to empty Miss Lillian's (Vyry's half sister) chamber pot. Big Missy (Salina) punishes Vyry by throwing the acrid content of the pot in Vyry's face and said, "There you lazy nigger, that'll teach you to keep your mind on what you're doing. Don't you let me have to tell you another time about this pot or I'll half kill you, do you hear me?" (p. 26). Her hatred for Vyry simmrs. Then, a few days later she hangs Vyry by the hands in a dark closet. Vyry, at the time, was seven years old. (So much for southern White womanhood.)

While all of this transpires, John Dutton is away on a trip. His daughter, Lillian, runs out to greet him upon his return home. She whispered in his ear, "Oh, Pappa, come quick, Vyry's hanging in the closet by her thumbs and I do believe she's dead" (p. 30).

John Dutton runs up the stairs and "rescues" Vyry. The exchanged heated words:

"What you trying to do, Salina, kill her?"

"Yes. I reckon that's what I oughta do. Kill her and all other yellow bastards like her. Killing's too good for her."

"Well, don't you try it again, dy'ye hear me? Don't you dare try it again! She's nothing but a child, but someday she'll be grown up and worth much as a slave" (p. 30).

This exchange captures the ambiguity of slavery. Although Vyry is his daughter, Dutton only sees her as potential valuable property. The tragic ambiguity of slavery is that he fails to see his own daughter as a person, although he does recognize her as a child, but a child of property.

Salina responds, "How much do you expect me to put up with? Here in this very house with my own dear little children. And my friends mortifying me with shame! Telling me she looks like Lillian's twin" (p. 31).

The White female felt guilt at the behavior of the White man's indiscretions, but the guilt was not directed at the cruelty of slavery but at the consequences of slavery. Often they responded with hatred toward the offspring of their mates rather than at the institution of slavery.

The question is: how did Vyry survive this pain and anguish? The answer would seem to lie with the other slaves like Aunt Sally who acted as surrogate parents and helped her. More often than not the slaves, although illiterate, responded to each other with kindness and sympathy. They also told them about "life."

It is Aunt Sally who explains to Vyry, for example, what menstruation means.

> It's what make you a woman. Makes you different from
> a no-good man. It's makes you grown up to have younguns
> and be a sho-nuff woman. A man ain't got the strength
> to have younguns. He too puny-fied. Man ain't nothing
> but trouble, just breath and britches and trouble. Don't
> let him feel over you, now, don't let a no-good man touch
> you, else he'll big you up sho-nuff (p. 45).

This attitude expressed by Aunt Sally seems too "modern" and more Margaret Walker speaking than Aunt Sally. The point made is that the slaves had a "community," responding to each other in times of need. One of the worst days in Vyry's life occurred when Aunt Sally was sold.

A technique that Walker uses throughout the novel is that of **contrast.** She contrasts the life of Vyry with that of her half sister, Lillian. Their lives are contrasted first because John Dutton accepts Lillian as his daughter whereas he rejects Vyry. Second, Salina treats the two radically different. With Vyry, there is unremitting hatred. For Lillian, there is in contrast, indulgence.

Nowhere is this technique of **contrast** more evident than in the court-ship patterns of Vyry and Lillian. When Vyry meets Randall Ware, a free Black man, freedom burns in her heart. She initially would not have anything to do with him. Later she falls in love with him. All day long she thought of nothing but Randall Ware and freedom (p. 79). She has to meet Randall Ware secretly at night in the corn fields.

In juxtaposition, Lillian has a "open" courtship with all the formalities. Kevin MacDougall, her beau, is brought to the house and introduced to the family. Lillian has a big wedding requiring months of prepara-tions.

The irony of the contrast is when Vyry finds herself pregnant and decides to go ask her father-master to marry Randall Ware. Vyry asks her father-master to marry and he says, "Oh, is that all...By the way, who do you want to marry? Is it one of my boys around here or a boy from a plantation somewhere around here?" (p. 119). When Vyry says "he free" (p. 119), John Dutton refuses to let her marry. Vyry sees her hope for freedom crushed. It is Randall Ware who keeps freedom before her as a dream. Vyry came to believe that freedom is a secret word she dare not say (p. 123).

Since Vyry cannot gain her freedom in any other way, she makes plans to escape reminiscent of Eliza in UNCLE TOM'S CABIN. The stipulation that Randall Ware makes is that Vyry leave her children behind. (These are the two children born by Vyry, Jim and Mirina.) Instead, she attempts to escape and gets bogged down in the mud. She is captured and given seventy-five lashes on her naked back (p. 142).

Portraying slavery from a personal perspective, Walker, though realistic, goes for the pathos. The sentimentality is tempered by the historical reality. Throughout the first part of the novel, Walker sets up the dominant theme of the book, the quest for freedom.

Freedom, of a sort, comes when the Union Army invades the south because of the Civil War. For the Dutton family, the war brings devastation and, in symbolic terms, the destruction of the southern aristocracy. There are several key incidents and losses for the Dutton family.

First of all, John Dutton has an accident, the carriage that he is riding in overturns, kills the driver, Sam, and smashes Dutton's leg. He refuses to have his leg amputated which leads to his death. His death causes a chain of mixed emotions and reactions in Vyry (p. 165). After all, it is her father.

Furthermore, when he had refused to let get married, he promised she would be free upon his death. Vyry does not expect anything from her father since he had done nothing for her in life.

A second incident that occurs is the death of Johnny Dutton who makes a dual journey to his home and to his burial place. The deaths of son and father has an incremental emotional toll on the family.

Third, Kevin McDougall is killed in the war. These losses cause Big Missy to become stoic, and she busies herself with the making of a confederate flag, gray with bars crossed and studded with stars (p. 211).

Lillian, on the other hand, becomes more hysterical and "dries" up emotionally. Not only do they lose their loved ones in the war, but they also lose the family fortune. In losing their fortune, they also lose their "status."

In addition, the slaves are running away in greater numbers. Big Missy summarizes much of the southern attitude when she says, "I tell you one thing, I never want to see the day when niggers are free and living like white folks" (p. 220). Salina has her wish; she has a massive stroke and dies before Lincoln issues the Emancipation Proclamation.

The death of her family has a traumatic emotional impact upon Lillian. She is alone in the world except for her half sister, Vyry. Lillian begins gradually to lose contact with reality. Lillian some days was dreamy-eyed and smiling, but most days she was too depressed to notice much of what was happening around her (p. 230).

Again, the contrast between the two characters, Vyry and Lillian, is made. Lillian deteriorates into a state of mental oblivion, whereas Vyry becomes stronger and in effect runs the Dutton household.

The Union Army invades the Dutton household and ransacks everything in sight. The final blow against Lillian's sanity is struck when a Union soldier hits Lillian in the head. It is Vyry who nurses Lillian back to health. It was not uncommon for the slaves to show compassion on their former masters. When everyone acknowledges that Lillian has lost her mind, relatives from Alabama come to take her.

Post-bellum freedom did not bring the "type" of freedom the Blacks thought. The South was devastated; it was a depressed area and exploited by the North. The Blacks found themselves as economically exploited after slavery as they were in slavery. The Ku Klux Klan rose; black codes were passed and Blacks were deprived of basic civil rights. Vyry found freedom to be a life of hard work. In place of slavery, another repressive economic system, sharecropping, replaced it. It rendered Blacks economically impotent. After waiting seven years, Vyry gives up hope that Randall Ware will return, therefore, she accepts Innis Brown's proposal of marriage.

45

Vyry finds herself with a new mate, Innis Brown, and a new baby. They have difficulties making a living and have to move twice in the novel. They are burned out by the Klan. The second time they have to move, Vyry decides that she wants to go see her half sister. She had not seen her for four years and she was shocked when she saw her. It wasn't just the fact that she was still wearing the old, out-of-date clothes she had before the war. It was mostly her frowsy hair and her empty eyes that disturbed Vyry. Miss Lillian did not recognize her when Vyry spoke, but she stood up and walked away from the rocking chair talking rapidly in a high childish treble and monotone. "I'm not crazy. I know who I am. I know my name. My name is Lillian..." Vyry began to cry (pp. 343-344).

What we need to keep in mind is that this is the story of two sisters, bound by the same father. In some sense, it is a metaphorical statement about the condition of Blacks and Whites in America. Not only are they citizens but they are also brothers and sisters.

To conclude the discussion of JUBILEE, we need to return to Randall Ware and discover what happened to him. We met Randall Ware at the beginning of the book as Vyry's lover and the father of her two children. If we remember, her father would not allow her to marry him. They had planned to escape, but Vyry was caught and she only sporadically heard from Randall Ware.

When the Union Army invaded the South, Randall worked as a blacksmith for the Northern army. He had tried to make it in the North but found that being free in the North was not much better than being free in the South. So he returned South.

Randall, although free, did like a lot of the Blacks; as many as possible fled to the Northern army. When he began to work as a Union blacksmith, in symbolic terms, he was in the war doing what he liked best, and striking a powerful blow for the freedom of Blacks (p. 189). His mind was always on freedom and Vyry.

Because she has children by Randall, she thinks of him from time to time and she keeps her promise to wait for him. After emancipation, she waits until she meets another man, Innis Brown. Again, Walker deploys the technique of contrast. Vyry compares Innis with Randall. Whereas Randall was jet black, Innis was light skinned. Randall was a skilled worker; Innis was a laborer. Second in importance to freedom, Randall was literate and Innis was ignorant.

Innis knew Vyry's heart was with another man, but he still asks her to come with him when Lillian's folks come to get her. "I dunno, I hasta think about it. Maybe, I dunno. If my husband ain't come by then, maybe so" (p. 252).

When Randall Ware has not returned after more then seven years, Vyry marries Innis Brown. Vyry leaves Georgia with her new family and goes to Alabama. Randall Ware comes for her, but it is too late. He finds out that Vyry has married. The rest of the novel juxtaposes two quests; the quest of Randall Ware for Vyry and Vyry's quest for a home.

Vyry has a baby, Harry, for Innis. Their lives are not easy. They have to make a living from the land, and Innis, like many of the newly freed Blacks, is illiterate and exploited by the Whites. They are turned out by the Klan. Meantime, Randall Ware is also forced to sell his land and move as well.

Vyry works for a while selling eggs. But the racist talk of the Whites is so upsetting that she stops that and becomes a midwife. They move for a third time and have their own home. This time they are not bothered by the Whites. This time the conflict is in her own family. Innis Brown realizes his dream as a farmer and he wants to make Jim, his stepson, a farmer also. It is clear that Jim is not cut out to be a farmer. He drives the young man mercilessly.

This brings up another theme in the novel, the theme of education. Vyry's dream is that her two oldest children go to school. She had heard of a school in Greenville, Alabama, but there was a tuition fee. She did not want to bring it up to Innis because she felt that he would not understand.

Then one day Vyry was sitting on her front porch teaching Minna how to piece quilts and showing her how to make tiny neat stitches. The little girl's eyes would frequently tire and wander away, and looking up she saw a man coming up the lane leading from the Big Road to their new farmhouse. Minna strained her eyes and looked again. "Maw, who is that? That's the blackest man I ever did see in my life!" (p. 388).

Of course, it was Randall Ware. Randall Ware brings dreams of education. He plans to take Jim back with him to attend a school in Selma, Alabama. Randall also questions the legality of Vyry's marriage to

Innis. "According to the law of Georgia, which regulated all slave marriages, she's still my wife, that is if she wants to be" (p. 391). The pivotal point is that they leave the decision to remain or to stay to Vyry.

In the final sections of the book, Innis and Randall's views on education are shown. Innis asks, "You thinks education gwine raise up the colored folks? I always been told education don't do nothing but make a nigger a fool" (p. 395). Randall replies.

> Well, that's the white man's attitude. He says an educated Negro gets ideas in his head about being free and equal.... When you can read and write and the white man can't make a fool out of you, he never likes it. You know it was against the law in slavery time to teach a black person to read or write. The white man must have had some fear about educating colored people or he wouldn't have had the law. He knows as long as we are ignorant people we are helpless (p. 395).

Randall Ware and Innis Brown represent the two strands of thought in Black intellectual history. To stretch the analogy, those two strands of thought are those of Booker T. Washington and W.E.B. DuBois. Or, if our imaginations are constrained, we can say that Randall Ware represents a progressive, militant point of view and Innis Brown suggests a reactionary passive type of mentality.

Randall Ware believes all White people hate Black people; he rejects Christianity; he castigates Vyry because she's half White and accuses her of loving "white folks bettern you love colored folks" (p. 397). When Vyry has heard enough from Randall, she reponds with a long speech.

> I ain't gwine try to beat the white man at his own game with his killing and his hating neither...You done called me a white folks' nigger and throwed up my color in my face cause my daddy was a white man. He wasn't no father to me, he was just my Marster. I got my color because this here is the way God made me (p. 405).

Vyry recounts her experiences with Big Missy, how she emptied Miss Lillian's pee-pot in her face, how she hung her up in the closet and worked her like a dog. "And worstest of all they kept me ignorant so's I can't read and write my name, but I closed her eyes in death, and God is my witness, I bears her no ill will" (p. 405).

Vyry represents a third point of view about the Black experience, that of the conciliatory Christian perspective. The leader who most admirably represented this position in the twentieth century was Martin Luther King, Jr.

Both men respond with marvel about Vyry, and they both know that she has made her choice. "Innis and me has got a marriage, Randall Ware. We has been through everything together, birth and death, flood and fire, sickness and trouble..." (p. 409). However, Vyry does allow Jim to go with his father to go to school and get an education. Education followed hard upon fredom as a priority of Blacks.

CHAPTER SIX

THE CONFESSIONS OF NAT TURNER: A STUDY IN AMBIGUITY

WILLIAM STYRON (1925-   )

William Sytron was born in Newport News, Virginia, in 1925, and
grew up in a nearby town listening to his grandmother's tales of her
slave-owning days. His first story appeared in a student collection
at Duke University, where he was a marine officer candidate. Sum-
moned to Okinawa, he arrived there bearing the fresh stripes of a
lieutenant, just as WWII was ending. Styron returned to Duke and
graduated in 1947. Later that year he moved to New York and enrolled
in Hiram Haydn's short story course at the New School. His work
there became part of his first novel, LIE DOWN IN DARKNESS (1951),
which brought him fame at the age of 26 when he was awarded the
Prix de Rome by the American Academy of Arts and Letters. Shortly
after, Styron moved to Paris where he helped found, together with
George Plimpton, Peter Matthiessen, and Donald Hall, the Paris Review. Before traveling on to Rome, Styron wrote, in one intense
six-week period during the summer of 1952, THE LONG MARCH.
His third novel, SET THIS HOUSE ON FIRE, based partly on Styron's
journey to Italy, was published in 1960. Seven years later, he completed
THE CONFESSIONS OF NAT TURNER, his brilliant and controversial
portrayal of the historical Black revolutionist, which won the 1967
Pulitzer Prize. After a long literary silence, Styron emerged with
another monumental work, SOPHIE'S CHOICE (1979), his impassioned
and emotionally devastating novel of a Holocaust survivor, and one
of the great critical and popular successes of recent years.

THE CONFESSIONS OF NAT TURNER, by William Styron, published in 1968 (Signet), was a book universally admired by European American critics and almost similarly disliked by Black American critics. A book that elicits such contradictory criticism is without doubt a powerful book.

The Black opposition falls into several areas. First, Black critics object to the book because they see it as **ahistorical.** They claim that Styron left out the fact that Nat Turner was married and Styron had him fantasizing about White females. Styron's rejoinder to this particular criticism is that he based his novel upon Nat's confession and in his confession Nat made no mention of a wife.

They also claim that Styron's assertion that the Nat Turner "rebellion" was the **only** sustained slave revolt in American history is fallacious. For the most part, they do not offer any counter evidence to destroy Styron's theses.

By all historical estimates (Aptheker, AMERICAN NEGRO SLAVE REVOLTS; John Hope Franklin, FROM SLAVERY TO FREEDOM), Turner's revolt is considered the most far-reaching slave revolt in American history. Exclusive of Nat Turner's Rebellion, the other two most notable slave revolts were those of Gabriel Prosser (1800) and Denmark Vesey (1822); neither of which came off because they were betrayed by fellow slaves, a key example of "brainwashing."

Today we know that Stanley Elkins' thesis that the plantation system created "Sambo" is not true because many of the slaves rebelled against slavery daily (Bauer p. 27). The most frequent type of rebellion was running away. So many of the slaves ran away that a second Fugitive Slave Law was passed in 1850. Instead of ending the running away, it intensified it. The Underground Railroad became even more active.

The point is that Nat Turner was the culmination of the slaves' dissatisfaction with slavery. Most slaves did not accept slavery but they remained slaves because the odds were too great that they could gain their freedom. It is testimony to the human spirit that so many ran or rebelled at all considering the fact that American slavery was such a totalitarian system.

The second criticism is that Nat was portrayed as a sexual pervert, pining after White women and that he engaged in a homosexual act in the book. There are two rejoinders to this criticism. The preoccupation of Black critics with the sexual passages in the book is clearly **hyperbolic.** The sexual passages in the book take up no more than an estimated ten pages in a 404 page book. The point missed by Black critics is that Styron is taking poetic license symbolizing Nat's sexual awakening. The homosexual encounter is followed by Nat's baptism and his baptism of Willis (pp. 198-204). Styron interweaves the themes of sex and religion, predominantly religion, throughout the novel.

Clearly, there is ambiguity here because it may be an imposition of White middle class cultural values on a Black situation. On the other hand, adolescents engage in homosexual play as part of their sexual awakening. More often than not, it is part of the rites of passage of adolescence.

A point overlooked by Black critics is that, for the most part, Nat is portrayed as a celibate. This state of celibacy allows Nat the energy to engage in his frequent meditation upon his "destiny." Mysticism is Nat's forte and not sexual deviation.

Styron claims that the Black male "obsession" with White females is part of the popular folklore. This "obsession" is written about most powerfully in Eldridge Cleaver's SOUL ON ICE.

For the most part, this is a myth because interracial liasons are the exception rather than the routine. Very few Black males prefer White females and ninety-nine percent of Black males who marry, marry Black females even today while it is legal to do so.

At the end of the novel, Black critics point out that Nat goes to his death thinking about Margaret Whitehead, the White girl who befriended him.

Black critics missed the thesis of the ending of the novel and the ideas that Styron conveyed. First of all, Nat expresses no remorse about what he has done. He says, "I would have done it all again. I would have destroyed them all. Yet I would have spared her that showed me Him whose presence I had not fathomed or maybe even known. Great God, how early it is! I had almost forgotten his name" (p. 403).

Singling out Margaret as Nat does is not because he loves her, but because she solidified for him the meaning of the love of God. In addition, she is the only person in the novel who sees Nat as a person.

It is not that Nat does not feel ambiguity toward Margaret. Earlier in the novel when Nat injures his hand, Margaret cries suddenly, "Your hand, it's bleeding!" (p. 323). When she attempts to minister to Nat, he jerks his hand away, fearful that a White woman shows him kindness. Nat thinks, "the rage returns and I can not tell why my heart is pounding so nor why my hatred for Margaret is, if anything, deeper than my hatred for her mother" (p. 234).

Nat hates Margaret but she has seen him as a person. He does not love her. Finally, as Nat proceeds to his death, he reconciles himself with God. These points Black critics seem to have missed.

There is a scene in the novel when Nat is in jail that does seem incredible; under the sentence of death, Nat has sexual revelries about a White female. It is doubtful that one will be thinking of sex before death and even more incredulous that a nineteenth century Black slave would be thinking of sex with a White woman before hanging. Perhaps Styron was trying to illustrate the absurdity of Nat's situation.

In Stephen Crane's "The Open Boat," the men are in a boat facing death and the cook begins to talk about pie. "Billie," he murmured, dreamfully, "What kind of pie do you like best?" "Pie!" said the oiler and the correspondent; agitatedly, "Don't talk about those things, blast you!" (Trachtenberg and Mott, p. 639). In the face of death, men are reduced to their most base levels; they think about the minimal necessities of life: food, water, and sex.

Lerone Bennett, Jr., points out another ambiguity in Styron's novel which is that Nat is portrayed as a hater of Black people. "The man erroneously and libelously identified as Nat Turner begins more and more to regard the Negroes of the mill and field as creatures beneath contempt," as "a lower order of people, a ragtag mob, coarse, raucous, clownish and uncouth" (Clarke, p. 9). In addition, Bennett attacks Styron for making Nat fantasize about being White. Although there is validity in Bennett's criticism, he, too, focuses too much on the sexual theme. As for the question of Black self hatred, it is there. It is manifested in the twentieth century by Black-on-Black crime. But Styron is right in that the desire to be White goes back to slavery.

It is seen in an early novel written by a Black, CLOTEL, OR THE PRESIDENT'S DAUGHTER, by William Wells Brown. Brown has a Black character, Sam, who was "one of the blackest men living...contended that his mother was a mulatto" (p. 100). Sam spent a great amount of time putting fresh butter on his hair to make it look like white people's hair, a practice some Blacks still engage in today.

In BLACK NO MORE, George Schuyler's satiric novel, he has a scientist discover a cure for Blackness and Blacks line up buying the product so they can turn White. Ralph Ellison ponders the same question more ambiguously in INVISIBLE MAN. Why do Whites want to tan themselves to become darker? And Blacks buy creams to make their skins whiter.

The point that Bennett overlooked is that these same people Nat held in disdain and contempt, he recruits as his lieutenants. Again, the Black critics missed a part of what Styron was trying to achieve and that is that Nat Turner did not organize an army because there were few Blacks he could trust because of their fear of White reprisal.

The Black critics tend to romanticize the Nat Turner rebellion in their criticism of Styron. They left many of the other questions of the novel to see if we can put some of the ambiguities in perspective.

To discuss a work of literature, one must be cognizant of literary terms such as style, structure, characterization and theme. Upon reading THE CONFESSIONS OF NAT TURNER, the first thing that strikes the reader is Styron's style. The book is written in two styles. There is the magnificent prose of Styron and then there is his "attempt" to write in the dialect of Nat Turner and the other Black slaves. When he is inside the mind of Nat Turner, he writes in "Standardized English." When he has Nat to talk, he writes in "Black dialect." Black critics attack his approach; however, I see it as a tour-de-force. Obviously, this is not the first time and perhaps not the last time that a European American will try to capture how Black people talk, although Black speech is as varied as White speech.

The most famous use of Black dialect with which I am familiar is Mark Twain's Huckleberry Finn. Many Blacks make the same mistake in attacking Twain as a racist as they do Styron when both men write explanations in the introductions. Twain says, "In this book a number of dialects are used, to wit: the Missouri Negro dialect; the extremist form of the back woods Southwestern dialect..." (Author's Note: THE ADVENTURES OF HUCKLEBERRY FINN). Styron says,

> I have rarely departed from the known facts about Nat Turner and the revolt of which he was the leader. However, in those areas where there is little knowledge in regard to Nat, his early life, and the motivations for the revolt (and such knowledge is lacking most of the time), I have allowed myself the utmost freedom of imagination in reconstructing events...it has been my intention to try to re-create a man and his era, and to produce a work that is less an 'historical novel' in conventional terms than meditation on history (Author's Note: THE CONFESSIONS OF NAT TURNER).

Like any author, Styron is personalizing his thoughts about an episode in American history. He does not try to write a "history" but only his reflections about that history. The end of the novel is a classic example of how Styron uses this technique. It is clear that he is using his imagination because he could not "know" what Nat was thinking before he died. He cannot be faulted for that; it is **only** a work of imagination.

Rather than discussing other elements of the novel, the complex structure, the outstanding style and the powerful characterizations, Black critics focused on those parts of the book that were less salient to the book.

The most powerful theme in the book, it seems to me, is Nat's **isolation.** The book begins with him alone in his prison cell, thinking about what he has done. Throughout his life, Nat is isolated because he is "different." Early in his life he was called to be a "prophet." His parents believed that he was "intended for some great purpose" (John Henrik Clarke, editor, WILLIAM STYRON'S NAT TURNER: TEN BLACK WRITERS RESPOND, p. 99).

He learns the alphabet through some miracle and learning becomes a part of his life. In the book, Nat is taught to read by one of his mistresses, Miss Nell. Even the Whites see that Nat is "different;" he is given better food than the field hands. Nat is, what is called in the vernacular, a "house nigger."

Nat, unlike the other Black males on the plantation, becomes celibate. He did not work like the others. Indeed, he had "leisure not granted to many other slaves" (p. 172). With this leisure, he threw himself into a study of the Bible. Miss Nell, furthermore, gives him a Bible one Christmas. His "difference" is emphasized when he says, "I must have been the (though unaware) only black boy in Virginia who possessed a book" (p. 173).

The key to understanding Nat Turner is that he had been proclaimed from an early age by both Whites and Blacks as someone "special." His "education" sets him apart from the other slaves.

The second thing that sets him apart is his **religious obsession.** Indeed, one of the points that Black critics missed is that Nat Turner is portrayed (and to me, rightly so) as a **religious fanatic.** Based upon his confessions, Nat is filled with the Spirit and visions. The most consequential vision that Nat has is "the appearance of the sign (the eclipse on the sun last February) I should arise and prepare myself, and slay my enemies with their own weapons" (Clarke p. 104).

Let me return to what I perceive as the dominant theme of the book, a discussion of isolation. Even when Nat organizes his "army," he is set apart from the men. He joins his men late on that fateful day.

There is considerable amount of ambiguity in both the confession and in the book about Nat's involvement in the massacre. As they go about their slayings, Nat follows. They garner more slaves; the slaves join them extemporaneously. The revolt is "organized chaos." Nat loses leadership of the group when a party of White men return with guns. His "army" disperses.

Some of what Styron writes about Nat Turner's revolt does portray his lack of understanding about Black psyche. For example, when he talks about the slaves joining Nat's army, he has a slave to say "I gwine git me some meat now--white meat. I gwine git me some dat white cunt too" (p. 358). In studies of American slave revolts, nowhere is it recorded that any slaves raped a white woman.

Styron portrays the "army" as filled with dissension. He sees some as motivated by rape which is not true. His most powerful depiction is the hatred, anger and outrage which the slaves feel toward Whites symbolized by Will.

Some of the slaves are drinking which Nat thoroughly rejects. When he sees one of them drinking, he knocks the bottle out of his hand. "No mo of that nigger. Applejack is out, you hear? I catch yo' black mouth at a bottle again and you goin' to get clobbered fo' good. Now git on back over there in the tree!" (p. 360).

Though courageous, they are a motley crew. I do not see anything wrong with this depiction. Regular organized armies have trouble in organization. In American Literature, this is portrayed by Stephen Crane in THE RED BADGE OF COURAGE. The foot soldiers are always complaining about the officers. Subordination and "frazzling" (beating officers) was a regular part of the Vietnam War. These are illiterate slaves; I do not see how one could expect anything less.

In addition, as I pointed out before, Nat's army was not really an "army." He began with an inner circle of four and as they went about their massacre, they added men as they went along. Some dropped by the wayside at the first sign of trouble, and they dispersed entirely when they met superior forces.

In the confession, Nat says (after his army was defeated) he believes that two of his men betrayed him. Next to his last stage of isolation on the gallows, Nat escapes into the woods. He says he would have stayed in the woods except for the fact that "two negroes" discovered him (Clarke, p. 112). When he told them who he was, they fled. "Knowing then they would betray me, I immediately left my hiding place, and was pursued incessantly until I was taken a fortnight afterwards by Benjamin Phipps" (Clarke, p. 112).

Thus ended the most famous slave revolt in American history. Thomas R. Gray, who recorded Nat's confession, has this to say about Nat.

> It has been said he was ignorant and cowardly, and that his object was to rob for the purpose of obtaining money to make his escape. It is notorious that he was never known to have a dollar in his life, to swear an oath, or drink a drop of spirits. As to his ignorance, he certainly never had the advantages of education, but he can read and write (it was taught him by his parents), and for natural intelligence and quickness of apprehension is surpassed by few men I have ever seen. He is a complete fanatic...The calm, deliberate composure with which he spoke of his late deeds and intentions, the expression of his friend-like face when excited by enthusiasm, still bearing the stains of the blood of helpless innocence about him...; I looked on him and my blood curdled in my veins (Clarke, p. 113).

This long quote captures the ambiguity of and about Nat Turner. In one instance, Nat is seen by the (White) public as ignorant and cowardly but Gray sees him as highly intelligent and brave, although from a White point of view, he has committed one of the most heinous acts in American history. He is one of the most moral men Gray has ever encountered, yet Nat commits the most immoral crime in the human experience and that is murder.

The ambiguity is also expressed by the use of the words "helpless innocence." From the Black perspective, the Whites are not innocent because they were slave holders engaging in the barbarous act of slavery. The Whites' vision is that Nat and his men were savages killing people.

Perhaps I can conclude by saying Nat Turner is an archetype and a symbol, although (because of the power of Styron) we get to know him as a person. The question becomes: What does Nat Turner symbolize?

Nat Turner represents the point of view of Blacks who believe that Black Americans can gain their freedom through violence. That his revolt failed suggests that violence is not the answer to Black Americans' problems. On the other hand, there is no question that many Black Americans are filled with rage and anger like Nat Turner, but often they turn this rage on to themselves. A final point to make about Nat Turner is that his revolt makes a statement about human nature. The nature of human beings is to be free. In his attempt to liberate his fellow slaves, Nat Turner was trying to liberate all humans. By trying to understand Nat Turner, we are attempting to arrive at the greatest human understanding, an understanding of ourselves.

REFERENCES

Aptheker, Herbert. AMERICAN NEGRO SLAVE REVOLTS. New York: Columbia University Press, 1943.

Bauer, Raymond and Alice. "Day to Day Resistance to Slavery." JOURNAL OF NEGRO HISTORY. October, 1942, p. 27.

Brown, William Wells. CLOTEL OR THE PRESIDENT'S DAUGHTER. New York: Macmillan Company, 1970.

Clarke, John Henrik, ed. WILLIAM STYRON'S NAT TURNER: TEN BLACK WRITERS RESPOND. Boston: Beacon, 1968.

Cleaver, Eldridge. SOUL ON ICE. New York: Dell, 1968.

Crane, Stephen. THE RED BADGE OF COURAGE. New York: Dell, 1960.

Crane, Stephen. "The Open Boat." Trachtenberg, Alan. AMERICAN LITERATURE, Volume Two. New York: John Wiley, 1978.

Elkins, Stanley M. SLAVERY: A PROBLEM IN AMERICAN INSTITUTIONAL AND INTELLECTUAL LIFE. New York: Universal, 1963.

Ellison, Ralph. INVISIBLE MAN. New York: Vintage, 1982.

Franklin, John Hope. FROM SLAVERY TO FREEDOM. Second ed. New York: Knopf, 1956.

Schuyler, George. BLACK NO MORE. New York: Macmillan, 1971.

Styron, William. THE CONFESSIONS OF NAT TURNER. New York: Signet, 1968.

Trachtenberg, Alan and Benjamin Mott. AMERICA IN LITERATURE, Vol. 2. New York: John Wiley, 1978.

Twain, Mark. ADVENTURES OF HUCKLEBERRY FINN. Second ed. New York: Norton, 1977.

WILLIAM STYRON: AN AMERICAN WRITER. Arts and Entertainment Network, 1985.

CHAPTER SEVEN

AMBIGUITY, IDENTIFICATION, AND RESISTANCE

IN A DIFFERENT DRUMMER

WILLIAM MELVIN KELLEY (1937-   )

Born in New York, Kelley was brought up in an Italian-American neighborhood in the North Bronx. He studied at Harvard under Archibald MacLeish and the novelist John Hawkes. Kelley has taught as a visiting professor at the New School for Social Research and the SUNY at Geneseo. In additon to A DIFFERENT DRUMMER, he has published DANCERS ON THE SHORE (1964), A DROP OF PATIENCE (1965), and DUNFORD TRAVELS EVERYWHERE (1970). Critics have notices the similarities between his work and that of Faulkner and Joyce.

Identification, ambiguity, and resistance are illustrated in William Melvin Kelley's A DIFFERENT DRUMMER. When Tucker Caliban decides to leave a mythical southern state and the rest of the Blacks follow him, Mr. Harper, one of the White men attempting to explain Caliban's militant spirit, says, "It's got to be the African's blood" (p. 16).

Then Mr. Harper tells the story of the African, Tucker Caliban's great-great-grandfather. He came off the slave ship rebelling. When he stepped off the ship, he was carrying a baby under his arm. Due to his immense physical strength, he had ripped the chains from the ship and used it as a weapon, killing the crewman. It took twenty men to subdue him. He had killed the crewman because the crewman had attempted to separate him from his baby.

The strategy that the auctioneers will use now is to sell them together. When the African was sold, the men relaxed his chains and the African sliced off the auctioneer's head with the chains in his hand. The African, along with the auctioneer's servant, runs with the chains and the baby. The African stays at bay for a month and then he returns and frees all of DeWitt Wilson's slaves and some slaves on other plantations.

Kelley suggests that, in the beginning of their experience in America, the newly arrived Africans and the American Blacks worked together for the cause of liberation. Kelley also includes the theme of ambiguity because a Black betrays the African's whereabouts. DeWitt Wilson, the owner of the African, asks why.

'Why'd you do this? Why'd you turn on him?' The Negro smiled again. 'I'm an American; I'm no savage. And besides, a man's got to follow where his pocket takes him, doesn't he?' (p. 29).

Kelley's position is that the ambiguity and identification with Africa began in slavery. At first, the auctioneer's slave identifies with the African, but his identification with American values are greater than his identification with the African, resulting in betrayal and ambiguity.

The hunters surround the African and his followers; they ask them to give up. The Black Americans immediately surrender, but the African fights alone. When he is mortally wounded, he picks up a rock to kill the baby, but DeWitt Wilson shatters the back of his head before he can kill the baby.

In this allegorical tale, Kelley has summarized many of the problems of the African-Black-American relationship. He implies that Black Americans have forgotten their African past. If they identified with their regal ancestry, they, too, would become that part of more militant. To some extent, the Blacks who rebelled in the sixties did identify with their African ancestry. The fact Kelley suggests is a true one; Africans rebelled before they got on the ships, after they were on the ships, in midpassage, and then they rebelled in American.

As seen by the betrayal of the auctioneer's slave, many Blacks betray their African heritage, identifying with the cultural values of American society, resulting in confusion about their identity.

REFERENCES

Kelley, William Melvin. A DIFFERENT DRUMMER. New York: Bantam, 1967.

Klotman, Phyllis R. "The Passive Resistance in A DIFFERENT DRUMMER, DAY OF ABSENCE, and MANY THOUSANDS GONE." STUDIES IN BLACK LITERATURE 3, iii 7-12.

Nadeau, Robert L. "Black Jesus: A Study of Kelley's A DIFFERENT DRUMMER. STUDIES IN BLACK LITERATURE 2, ii 13-15.

CHAPTER EIGHT

THE AUTOBIOGRAPHY OF MISS JANE PITTMAN:

A STUDY IN LEADERSHIP

Ernest J. Gaines (1933-   )

Born in Oscar, Louisiana, Ernest J. Gaines worked on a plantation. In 1948, the family moved to Vallejo, California, seeking greater opportunity. He graduated from San Francisco State College, receiving a B.A. in 1957. He did graduate work at Stanford University in the fiction workshop. In addition to THE AUTOBIOGRAPHY OF MISS JANE PITTMAN, Gaines has written three other novels, CATHERINE CARMIER (1964), OF LOVE AND DUST (1967), and BLOODLINE (1968). One of the themes of Gaines' work is Black life in rural Louisiana.

THE AUTOBIOGRAPHY OF MISS JANE PITTMAN traces the life of Jane Pittman, born in slavery, until the sixties. It is not a book about slavery but more about the historical period beginning with the end of slavery to the civil rights movement of the sixties.

In this novel, the reader gets to see the end of slavery, its aftermath, and the Civil Rights movement of the sixties. The novel gives the reader insights into the historical circumstances of the newly freed slaves.

The novel starts with the Civil War and the invasion of the Northern troops in the South. Jane Pittman is a child. Her task, at the beginning of the novel, is to serve water to the retreating Southern army.

Gaines portrays slavery as brutal. Jane Pittman's mistress beats her until she bleeds and threatens to sell her. "Who go'n buy her with them yankees tramping all over the place?" my master said (p. 9).

When Jane is ten or eleven, the Emancipation Proclamation is issued. When the slaves were freed, they exulted but later they asked the question, "Master, if we free to go, where is we to go?" (p. 11).

Booker T. Washington describes a similar scene in his autobiography, UP FROM SLAVERY. He says when the slaves received news of their freedom, they shouted and jumped enthusiastically. But then a depression set in because now they had to fend for themselves.

Some of the slaves remained on the plantation. Others left the plantation, but they had no idea where they were going. The idea is that the slaves were almost totally unprepared for freedom. Some, like Jane Pittman, left the plantation going North. She says, "We didn't know a thing. We didn't know where we was gling, we didn't know what we was go'n eat when the apples and potatoes ran out, we didn't know where we was go'n sleep that night" (p. 16). They just started walking. In fact, many of the slaves did not have last names. They made them up, generally taking the last names of their masters.

According to Gaines, the newly freed slaves not only had the problem of geography but they also had to face violence from less than liberal Whites. There is a scene in the novel where the newly freed slaves are violently assaulted by poor White trash called "Patrollers" who used to find runaway slaves. When they saw the former slaves, they massacred them. A few were left alive. Among them were Jane and her adopted son, Ned. They kept going in the direction which they thought was North. Instead, they wind up in "Luzana." It is in Louisiana that Jane sets her roots.

Therefore, the former slaves faced several problems. The first was the problem of survival. To survive, they found themselves working again for Whites. During post-slavery, a new economic system was introduced in the South which was not far removed from the system of slavery itself. That system was "sharecropping."

The Blacks would work for Whites and share what they picked. They would live on the owner's land, work the land, and had to pay a "share" of their earnings to the owner. They remained constantly in debt.

A second problem which was more important was education. The former slaves thirsted after education. Congress created the Freedmen's Bureau to educate them. The South created all kinds of barriers to make it difficult for the former slaves to become educated. After reconstruction, the South, with the aid of the Supreme Court decision in 1896, came up with the idea of "separate but equal." The segregation of races remained the law of the land until 1954.

Gaines takes us from the end of slavery to the sixties. He interweaves a story mixed with politics, education, rebellion, violence, the rise of the Ku Klux Klan, and the rise of the civil rights movement.

To conclude this brief narrative, let us look at one of the central characters of the novel, Ned Douglass, who is a prototype of the Black leader.

At the beginning of the novel, Ned is a little boy whose parents were killed and he is "adopted" by Jane, who was just a child herself. New grows to manhood and decides to become a leader of his people. New joined a committee fighting for Blacks' rights because Blacks and Whites were discovering that Blacks were no better off than they were in slavery. He changed his last name to Douglass after the great nineteenth century Black leader, Frederick Douglass.

Ned left home, went to Kansas, and worked for Black rights in Kansas. New attained an education, went into the army, and became a teacher. He returned to Louisiana to organize and to teach his people. New organizes a school to teach Blacks about themselves and about their history.

67

He is the prototype of the Black leader. He receives an education like Frederick Douglass, and he begins to agitate for the rights of Blacks. Like most educated Black males, he is considered a "threat" by the White community.

When Jane tells his wife of Albert Cluveau's threats to kill him, Ned continues to speak out. He preaches a sermon beside the river. He says, "I'm much American as any man; I'm more American than most" (p. 109). He speaks out against the teaching of Booker T. Washington. He teaches the people the distinction between "black men and niggers" (p. 112). After his "sermon," he says to Jane, "I'm go'n die, mama." But I knowed he had no fear of death (p. 112).

Later, he is assassinated. His career parallels the careers of most Black leaders. He educates himself, then he educates his people. When he becomes a threat to the White community, he is slain. Martin Luther King Jr.'s career is a classic example. As Joseph Lowrey said in an interview on Sunday Morning, the CBS news program, "Everything has changed and nothing has changed" (January 19, 1986).

REFERENCES

Bryant, Jerry H. "From Death to Life: The Fiction of Ernest J. Gaines." IOWA REVIEW 3 (1972): 106-120.

Gaines, Ernest. THE AUTOBIOGRAPHY OF MISS JANE PITTMAN. New York: Bantam, 1967.

Lowery, Joseph. Quoted Sunday Morning CBS News (January 19, 1986).

Stoelting, Winifred L. "Human Dignity and Pride in the Novels of Ernest Gaines." CLAJ 14:340-358.

CHAPTER NINE

AMBIGUITY, IDENTIFICATION, AND QUEST IN ROOTS

ALEX HALEY (1922-)

Alex Haley was born in Henning, Tennessee, the son of a college professor. He attended college for two years, and he enlisted in the Coast Guard at seventeen. To alleviate the boredom, he began to write letters, to read extensively, and to prepare himself for a career as a journalist. He remained in the Coast Guard for twenty years, became eligible for retirement, and began his career as a writer, working for the Reader's Digest writing biographies. He did a series of interviews for Playboy Magazine which led to an interview with Malcolm X. This led to the book, THE AUTOBIOGRAPHY OF MALCOLM X (1963), which brought him his initial fame. ROOTS, his second book, was made into the miniseries which became the most watched television program in American television history.

The television program "Roots" remains the most watched television program in American history. It was based upon the novel, ROOTS, by Alex Haley. The story is, by now, well know. Kunta Kinte, in America, tries to maintain his African past, but his attempt to cling to his African heritage is continually assaulted by American culture and rejection by the fellow slaves. By constant retelling of the story of where he came from, Kunta Kinte's heritage is passed down from the beginning of his family's sojourn in America to his distant ancestor Alex Haley. Alex Haley, through a constant and diligent search, finds his long lost relatives.

For the sake of documenting AMBIGUITY AND IDENTIFICATION, it would be fruitful to briefly outline the structure of the novel and to analyze the relationship of Kunta Kinte to characters in the book.

There are four general parts to ROOTS; one is the story of Kunta Kinte, his life in Africa and his capture and enslavement in America. The second part of the story examines the life of his daughter, Kizzy, her adolescence, her sale into slavery, and the birth of her son, Chicken George. The third part of the story deals with Chicken George and his struggle to gain his family's freedom. The fourth part concerns itself with Chicken George and Alex Haley's quest.

Kunta Kinte's relationship to "toubob land," or America, begins with his sale into slavery. He attempts to escape four times. His first relationship is to a slave named Samson who calls him "Toby" for the first time. The first way in which the African heritage of Kunta Kinte is destroyed is to define him as property. In a sense, renaming is symbolic of taking away his African identity.

After he escapes for the last time, his foot is cut off. Ali A. Mazrui says, "by losing his foot he was brutally cut off from his historical past" (p. 8). Bell, the cook of the Waller plantation, nurses him back to health. He does not initially develop a relationship with her beyond nurse-patient. Later, this becomes his most important relationship.

It is in his third relationship, which is the second most important, that we see the ambiguity-identification paradigm established and that is in his relationship to Fiddler. It is Fiddler's task to "American-ize" Kunta. Fiddler tells him what America is like. After he gives Kunta a litany of negative laws about Black-White relationships, Fiddler says, "Dey's even a law 'gainst niggers beating any drums--any dat African stuff" (p. 274).

In other words, Fiddler tells him attempting to be an African is against the American legal system. When he sees Kunta Kinte fingering his tribal saphie charm, Fiddler says, "See what I mean? You got to put away all dat stuff...Give it up. You ain't goin no wheres, so you might's well face facks an' start fitting in, Toby, you hear?" (p. 275).

Fiddler, the pragmatic realist, tries to tell Kunta Kinte to forget about Africa. Kunta Kinte reacts angrily when he is called "Toby" and he says, "Kunta Kinte," Fiddler says, "Looka here, he can talk! But I'm telling you, boy, you got to forgit all dat African talk. Make white folks mad and scare niggers..." (p. 276). The ambiguity is expressed by the fact that White folks do not want the Blacks to retain their African heritage and the Blacks, out of fear, acquiesce in forgetting about Africa.

Kunta Kinte, however, does not forget about Africa; he keeps up with age by dropping small pebbles in a gourd, a Mandinka custom. The chief process of his Americanization is to learn English taught to him by Fiddler. Although he remembers his African heritage, slowly he becomes Americanized. First he becomes a gardener, learning an American vocation; then he learns the trade of a buggy driver. When he courts Bell, he does it in part through his African heritage; he gives Bell a pestle and a mortar and a Mandinka mat. However, when he gets married, he does not marry according to the tradition of Africa, but he "jumps the broom," an American slave custom.

It is in his relationship to Bell that we see the ambiguity-identification complex more clearly. Like Fiddler, she identifies with Kunta Kinte the person, but she does not identify with his "Africaness." When he tells Bell that she reminds him of a Mandinka woman, "'What fool stuff you talkin' bout?' she said irately. 'Don' know how come white folks keep on emptin' out boatloads a you Africa niggers!'" (p. 295).

It is clear she separates herself from Africans; she does not understand them. After Kunta Kinte told her she looked like a Mandinka woman, she wouldn't speak to him for a month. The silence is broken because of the outbreak of the American Revolution, the news of which Bell wants to share with Kunta.

As Kunta gets older, he starts to think about marriage. Two women come to mind; first, he thinks of Liza but something held him back from pursuing a relationship with her. "Then one night, while he was lying in bed trying to sleep, it struck him like a lightning bolt! There was another woman he might consider; Bell" (p. 334).

I have alluded to Kunta Kinte's courtship pattern; it was part African and part American. When they got married, it troubled him that they did not get married through the rituals of Africa but by "jumping the broom." Their marriage is relatively compatible with Bell satisfying most of his needs and he satisfying hers as well. It is, however, not a marriage without conflict. The conflict, inevitably, is centered around Kunta Kinte's attempts to maintain his African heritage. When their daughter is born, the problem of naming her crystallizes the conflict. It infuriated Kunta that his daughter would always have the last name of her master but "he searched his mind for a name, some Mandinka word," that would connect her to her African heritage (p. 360).

Kunta tells Bell that naming a child by the father is the way they did things in Africa and that he wanted to give their daughter a name before the master gives her some meaningless toubob name.

> 'Now I see!' said Bell. 'Dese Africanisms you so full of ain't gon' do nothin' but make trouble. An' day ain't gon' be none of dem heathen ways an names, neither, for dis child!' (p. 365).

Kunta does not understand how the Blacks in America could cut themselves off so completely from Africa which had been the source of their being. His anger and rage is directed not only at the "toubobs," but also at the Black Americans. He was determined that he would give his own child a name.

Bell comes to him to explain why she acted so harshly against him naming the child.

> 'Look here, Kunta,' she said, '...it's somethings I known 'bout massa bettr'n you does. You might git him mad wid that African stuff, he sells us all three at de next county seat auction jes' sho's we born' (p. 367).

In other words, Bell operates on the principles of compromise and accommodation. Compromise and accommodation are ambiguous activities. She finally acquiesces to Kunta naming their baby. She sees the African ritual of naming children as "mumbo jumbo" (p. 367).

One of the dominant images of the television program, "Roots," is when Omoro raises **Kunta** Kinte, as an infant, above his head under the moon and stars and names him. Kunta Kinte repeats the ritual in America. He takes his baby, raises her above his head "and then slowly and distinctly, he whispered three times into the tiny ear, 'Your name is Kizzy. Your name is Kizzy. Your name is Kizzy'" (pp. 367-368). As he begins to walk back to Bell and his cabin, he stopped and raised Kizzy again "to the heavens and this time he spoke aloud to her in Mandinka: 'Behold, the only thing greater than yourself!'" (p. 368).

Kunta was immensely satisfied. His child would only have one touob name. When he returns to Bell, he tells her that their child is named "Kizzy," which means to "stay put." "Stay put but don't stay a slave." It is up to Bell to get the master to accept the name. The master comments that it is an "odd name" but he had nothing against it. Then, he wrote in his Waller Bible: "Kizzy Waller, born September 12, 1790" (p. 369).

Ambiguity and identification are apparent in this African ritual of naming. Bell identifies with Kunta but she has to compromise both with him and the master to get her child named. The ambiguity is present in that Kizzy has both an African and an American name. After the television episode, there was a plethora of Black Americans naming their children "Kunta Kinte." For the most part, most Black Americans have two American names.

The narrative begins to turn to a discussion of Kizzy's life. Kizzy is also caught up in the conflict of ambiguity. She is influenced by four forces. First, her mother, Bell, raises her to be as "house nigger," accepting White values and culture in order to survive. Second, she comes under the influence of Missy Anne, the niece of Master Waller. As they grow up together, they are friends and playmates. Third, she comes under the influence of her father, who teaches her about her African past through language and stories. Finally, she comes under the influence of Noah, the field hand, with whom she falls in love.

Let me attempt to show how these forces shape Kizzy's life. When Kizzy is growing up, she is befriended by Missy Anne who teaches her to read, and when they are young, they are friends. As they grow older, the unwritten code is that a White girl and a Black girl must not be friends because it smacks too much of equality.

But before they reach that point, Kizzy is always with Missy Anne, to the consternation of her father.

> It filled him with revulsion to see his little girl being patted, kissed, or fondled by the massa's niece. It reminded him of an African saying, 'In the end, the cat always eats the mouse it's played with' (p. 371).

Kunta's concern for his daughter is an example of foreshadowing; his anxiety and his daughter's devourment by the White world will come to pass. Kunta has to share his daughter with both Missy Anne and Bell. Bell, the optimist and compromiser, tries to tell him no harm can come of this relationship. Kunta cannot bring himself to believe it.

Kunta resents the fact that his daughter is more influenced by American culture than his African heritage. Nowhere is this more dramatically illustrated than on Kizzy's second birthday. He learns that Kizzy will spend most of her birthday with Missy Anne. Kunta is furious but Bell calms him down by telling him that she feels the same way but she says, "I ruther dis dan her growin' up a fiel' han' youngun..." (p. 384). Again, Kunta acquiesces for he does not want to sentence his daughter to a life as a field hand.

To transmit his African heritage to his daughter, he teaches her the Mandinka language. When Bell learns that he has been teaching Kizzy Mandinka, she explodes.

> 'Ain't you got no sense at all, man?' she shouted. 'Don't you better pay me 'tention--git dat chile an' all us in bad trouble wid dat mess! You better git in you hard head she ain't no African!' (pp. 386-387).

Kunta, the narrative explains, never came so close to striking Bell. How could these people, he thought, be so ashamed and disdainful of their heritage? What is the matter with them?

Another incident shows Kunta how the Black Americans, even his own family, have rejected their African heritage. Kizzy gets sick and Missy Anne brings her a doll. Kunta had made Kizzy a Mandinka doll for her birthday but he had never given it to her. When he brings her the doll, she likes it and even Bell admires it. "But Kunta could see, after a few minutes, that Kizzy liked the toubob doll better, and for the first time in his life, he was furious with his daughter (p. 387).

The fact that Kizzy likes the toubob doll better symbolizes her alienation from Africa. To Kunta's frustration and amazement, Bell encourages Kizzy to forget about Africa. Bell's position is that "dem Africa things brings troubles" (p. 389).

The sense of outrage and impotency which Kunta feels is difficult to describe. Their conflict in the rearing of their daughter suggests the conflict between Black Americans' feelings for their African past. Most, like Bell, want no part of it, and others, like Kunta, want them to retain their African heritage.

There are three other examples where Kunta sees his daughter becoming an American. One is in the area of religion. Kunta Kinte remains a Moslem, praying to Allah, but his daughter, through her mother, becomes a "Christian." Missy Anne has asked Kizzy to go to church with her. Bell tells Kunta that she has to be christened first in their church. Kunta does not understand what "christen" means. When she tells him that it means to join the church, Kunta says, "Den she ain't gwine no church." Bell replies, "You still don' understan' does you African? It's a priv'lege to be axed to day church. You say no de nex' thing you an' me both out pickin' cotton" (p. 392).

Bell accepts White categories whereas Kunta rejects them. This is a perennial conflict in the Black American experience. The two points of view represented here are those of assimilation and cultural pluralism; those Blacks who say they are Americans and those who say they are African-Americans.

When Kizzy is baptized, Kunta stops it because he thinks she is being drowned. Bell explains to the minister, "It's awright, reveren'. Dat's jes' my African husban'. He don't unnerstan'. I 'splain to him later. You go ahead" (p. 392).

Slowly and relentlessly, the Africans, as symbolized by Kunta, lose their African heritage. Bell trains Kizzy to be a "house nigger" and Kunta teaches her about Africa. When he is alone with Kizzy, he teaches her the African language and about her people in Africa. He also teaches her that she is a human being.

Kunta, symbolic of African culture, acts as counter-alternative to the teachings of Missy Anne and Bell, who symbolize American culture.

As far as possible, he teaches her about Africa through language and through some of the customs he has retained such as dropping pebbles into a gourd to count her age.

Missy Anne has taught Kizzy to read and write and this will prove to be her downfall. Kizzy, as far as she can, teaches her parents to read. This is definitely a Black American tradition and has remained so until the nineteen sixties when public schools began to integrate. Many Blacks left teaching and the teaching of Blacks, except in historically Black colleges, as the domain of Whites.

Kunta worries about the physical maturing of Kizzy. She is now becoming interested in boys, particularly Noah. Her mother is concerned about it too. "You listen here, gal, don' you never lemme hear 'bout you fanning your tail roun' dat Noah no mo'! I take a hik'ry stick to you in a minute" (p. 440). Bell's concern is more about class; she does not want Kizzy to become involved with a field hand. Kunta's concern, on the other hand, is about whether his daughter will produce a baby by a White man. At least with Noah, their baby will be Black. "He realized he wasn't feeling very African about it..." (p. 450). He just didn't want his daughter with a big belly before she got married.

All of the thinking about Kizzy's fate goes for naught because Noah runs away. When he is captured, it is discovered that Kizzy wrote the pass. Despite the fervent pleas by her parents, Master Waller sells Kizzy. Although Bell has worked for him for forty years, he responds "glacially. The law is the law. She's broken my rules...She's going to be sold--that's all there is to it" (p. 452).

When his daughter is sold, Kunta scooped "up the double handful containing those footprints...The ancient forefathers said that precious dust kept in some safe place would insure Kizzy's return to where she made the footprints." He goes inside to find a place to put the dust and then he realizes Kizzy is not coming back. He drops the dust on the floor and smashes the gourd that records his age. In these symbolic acts, Kunta Kinte is finally defeated by American culture. The traumatic effect of losing Kizzy, symbolic of losing his African heritage, causes him to die a short time later according to the television. In the novel, this is not made explicitly clear.

In ROOTS, we see how the culture of the Africans was systematically destroyed in America. This was done through a number of steps. First, the African was forcibly removed from his homeland. Second, he was defined as less than a human being causing all kinds of psychological trauma. Third, his name and language were stripped from him. His identity was reforged on American shores. Because he lost his Islamic or African religion, he had to create a new one. Through the reading of ROOTS, one can see the shallowness of the argument that Black Americans are still Africans.

James Baldwin says, "one wonders what on earth the first slave found to say to the first dark child he bore" (p. 144). Alex Haley shows that his family told them stories of their African heritage.

Alex Haley's journey was a metaphorical one. His identification with Africa and his quest for his ancestors symbolizes not only the quest of Black Americans for their "roots," but also the quest of all men and women. When one looks back at the phenomenon of "Roots," there has never been an event which raised more hope for easing race relations. Vernon Jordan called it the most significant civil rights event since the march on Selma in 1965. Many saw it as an opportunity for more a "realistic" portrayal of Blacks on television. Haley said he hoped "Roots" would help Blacks develop pride in themselves and buoy up their self esteem. Some saw it as a foundation for increased interest in Africa and Black studies.

"Roots," however, was not without its detractors. Two lawsuits were filed against Alex Haley by Harold Courlander and Margaret Walker who accused Haley of plagiarism. He settled out of court with Courlander and the suit by Walker was dismissed.

Other criticism about "Roots" centered around historical inaccuracies. The type of slavery depicted in "Roots" was not endemic to Virginia. Slavery was not that harsh in Virginia, many historians claimed. The slavery portrayed in "Roots" was more peculiar to the deep southern states; i.e., Alabama and Mississippi.

Cotton was not widely grown in Virginia but tobacco. During the time depicted in "Roots," there was a war going on between the English and a local chief, so no man would have come near Kunta Kinte's village. Haley was also criticized for a romantic portrayal of Africa.

The most consistent criticism of "Roots" was that it was a "T.V. soap opera for the middle brow." The program had all the elements of melodrama with caricatures portrayed rather than real people. The Blacks were depicted as heroic and the Whites were consistently villains. Many people even criticized the "casting," particularly those of O.J. Simpson, Leslie Uggams, and Ben Vereen. O.J., some said, looked like he was still playing halfback for the Buffalo Bills. Leslie Uggams had her beautiful fingernails. Ben Vereen, as Chicken George, was criticized because he is as old as Leslie or older and some asked how could he be the product of a Black woman and a White man and not be a mulatto.

These criticisms notwithstanding, "Roots" was a profound and traumatic experience for many Americans. The central question we need to ask remains does it make a difference for Black Americans to trace their ancestry to Africa?

Benji J. Anosike asks the same question. He says there are three reasons why Black Americans need to identify with Africa; they are **psychological, political,** and **sociological.** The psychological includes the inner satisfaction of knowing where one came from. For Black Americans, it is more of a powerful impulse because "collective amnesia" has been imposed upon them. They, as we have shown, have been forced to forget their past. By knowing something of their past, they can feel that they, too, have a history.

In terms of politics, they can identify with the power of Africa; they can see Black members of OPEC; they can see Black ambassadors from other countries and Black heads of state, and they can, perhaps, attempt to connect their bourgeoisie political power with that of their Black brothers and sisters in Africa.

Sociologically, they can see that Africa had an organized and highly complex society before and after the White man's sojourn in Africa. This society was dominated by strong respect for family, elders, and religion. Despite knowing all of this and knowing about Africa, the evidence comes down hard that Black Americans are Americans and not Africans.

Anosike goes on to say that:

> Africa and her American descendants would be in a position to attain the highest levels of mutual understanding and solidarity in their interactions when and only when one precondition is met, namely, when the Afro-American shall have started to transmute his 'American mentality,' the automatic, across-the-board attraction, conscious

or unconscious, of all things white or Western, so that the cultural elements of the Afro-American's Africaness...is accommodated. When the Afro-American shall have ceased to be (culturally) '100 percent American,' but perhaps just 10-25 percent African, only then would the two people enjoy the best of relationships (p. 448).

REFERENCES

Anosike, Benji, J.O. "Africa and the Afro-American: The Bases for Greater Understanding and Solidarity," JOURNAL OF NEGRO EDUCATION, Volume 51, No. 4.

Baldwin, James. NOTES OF A NATIVE SON. New York: Bantam Books, 1972.

Haley, Alex. ROOTS. New York: Dell, 1977.

Mazrui, Ali. "Roots - The End of American Amnesia," AFRICAN REPORT, May-June, 1977.

CHAPTER TEN

THE LEGACY OF SLAVERY

There is considerable debate today about the status of the Black family. Some have argued that the Black family was destroyed during slavery. That may be true, but Gutman's book disputes this. By examining the court records of New York and other states, Gutman found a remarkable stability of Black families during and after slavery.

Many Black Americans, including myself, can point to long-term marriages in our kinship structure. If one can argue that slavery destroyed the Black family, one must also account for the period from 1863-1963, a period in which there was relative stability of the Black family.

The breakdown of the Black family began late, after World War Two. It correlates to the movement of Blacks from the rural South to the urban North. E. Franklin Frazier documents this in his book, THE NEGRO FAMILY IN THE UNITED STATES.

The dominant force which contributed to the breakdown of the Black family after World War Two and prior to the sixties has been **economics.** One could argue that because of job discrimination, many Black males were unable to get jobs to support their families. Some walked out, leaving the mothers dependent on increasing government programs.

One of the ironies of the welfare systems is that in sheer numbers there are more Whites on welfare than Blacks. In terms of proportion, the disproportioned number of people on welfare are Black women and their children.

One can argue that this has nothing to do with slavery. There are other forces at work; the most significant is the technological revolution which took place after World War Two. Because of the massive introduction of machines into the marketplace, a number of "types" of jobs declined or disappeared altogether. In my youth, men could work as janitors for a lifetime and support their families on a modest level. Today, one cannot aspire to be a janitor for his vocational career.

Jobs for pullman porters, ditch diggers, and garbagemen declined or disappeared from the economy. In addition, there was increasing emphasis on the high school diploma as a minimal credential for entry into the labor market. Jobs emphasizing brawn declined in favor of jobs based on skills or brains. Black Americans got caught up in a **technological revolution.**

But slavery did leave some legacies. Seemingly, the most profound problem Black Americans have as a result of slavery is **psychological.** The question one must ask is: how do Blacks feel about each other and how do they behave toward one another?

The evidence is ambiguous. Following the American way, Blacks saw the need for self-help organizations. They established churches, fraternal organizations, business coops, insurance companies, burial societies, and many other social groups. They still continue this tradition today.

Yet, other organizations have replaced the church as the focal point of many Black Americans' lives. For young Black males, the street and the athletic fields have become paramount in their lives. Because of the technological changes which I have alluded to, **crime** became an alternative for many Black males as a vocation.

Black Americans, early in their experience, developed **social class.** This social class was based on differentiation in jobs, property, slave or free status, and color. Until the sixties, light-skinned Blacks thought they were better than dark-skinned Blacks. This can be traced back to slavery. This is a classic example of **brainwashing.**

The light-skinned Blacks who were products, more often than not, of the White males' lust took pride in the fact that they had "White blood," or "good hair."

One of the legacies lost during the last generation is the high value Blacks used to place on education. The drop-out rate for Black youths is at an estimated national average of fifty percent. They do not stay in school. James Baldwin puts it this way when someone told him he should go to college. He said, "I had seen too many college educated handymen." Many Blacks echo his sentiment. That, for many Blacks, is a fatal mistake. Every ethnic group which has made it in American society has made it primarily through **education, the mastery of language,** and **knowledge of books.** Blacks, somewhere, have lost this.

Some things have happened in the last generation which the ancestors of Black Americans could only dream. Nat Turner would probably turn over in his grave sans skin and all if he knew today that a Black is lieutenant-governor of the state of Virginia.

Even Blacks who lived through segregation would be surprised that there are no signs in the south saying "White," or "Colored." That, routinely, Blacks are addressed as "Sir" or "Madam" when engaging in marketplace transactions. Couples today interracially marry, even in the Deep South.

Despite the progress that Black Americans have made, they still remain near the bottom of the socio-economic ladder in American society. Scholars, intellectuals, and lay people reflect on the question: why other ethnic groups have "made it" but Blacks have not?

Black Americans have been freed from physical slavery but are still enslaved **culturally** and **psychologically.** Black Americans have an ambiguous vision about themselves in American culture.

During slavery, they were seen as sports figures and as entertainers for Whites. In "the battle royal" scene in INVISIBLE MAN, Ellison captures this image.

The narrator, Jack-the-bear, thinks he has been invited to give a speech before the most influential Whites of his community who he thinks are impressed with his "brain power." Instead, the main event is a "battle royal" in which he and several of his companions fight blindfolded in the ring. Their chief purpose is to entertain the Whites. Ellison captures this ignominious purpose through boxing, both entertainment and sport for Whites.

Arthur Ashe has edited and compiled a history of the Black athlete. In the early part of the twentieth century, Blacks were thought not to possess the courage or physical stamina to become great athletes. Today the image of the Black athlete is just the opposite. Black Americans are thought of primarily as athletes because they are nearer the animals.

When Bill Russell, the former great center of the Boston Celtics who led them to eleven championships, was asked why so many blacks make it in professional basketball after someone had written in Sports Illustrated that the stronger Blacks were imported from Africa, he answered with one word, "practice." Blacks are not "natural" athletes or singers. Those who achieve in those areas do so because they practice.

Black-on-Black crime is a twentieth century phenomenon. Black slaves did not injure each other in the manner that "free" Blacks do today. Most Blacks believe that Black Americans, particularly Black males, are economically frustrated; therefore, they turn to crime more often against each other. Black-on-Black crime is an issue in which Black leaders are devoting considerable energy combatting.

Part of the problem that Black Americans have is related to the racist nature of the American criminal justice system. Less value is placed on a Black life than a White. When Blacks commit crimes against a Black, they are given a more lenient sentence than when they engage in crimes against Whites.

Black Americans, or more specifically poor Black Americans, still face difficulties in getting decent housing. The question today is whether or not housing discrimination is economic or racial. The evidence suggests that it is both but economics is more powerful than race.

At every level, economics and race go together and one becomes confused as to which is more powerful. It is part of what James Baldwin calls "paranoia." He says the racial situation in American is intense enough to make the most balanced of Blacks lose his mental stability.

Black Americans, as a group, are in bad shape compared to other Americans. They suffer the worst that America has to offer. They have the highest mortality rate, suffer the most from an assortment of diseases; cancer, heart attack, suicide, and hypertension. Their numbers in higher education are declining. By 1990, seventy percent of Black children will be born out of wedlock, indicating a precarious future for the group.

Yet, there is hope despite these dismal facts. Many Blacks, during the sixties and seventies, earned M.B.A.'s and are now leaving the corporations to form their own businesses. This can only have positive effects in the future.

Blacks are beginning to turn their energies to their own problems. Many Blacks are beginning to say that Black Americans should take responsibility for their own problems.

With the rich history that Black Americans have, they can look to their ancestors as models for their future. If an ethnic group can survive American slavery, it can survive anything. James Baldwin said it best in THE FIRE NEXT TIME. He wrote a letter to his nephew saying, "you come from a long line of great poets, some of the greatest poets since Homer. One of them said, 'the very time I thought I was lost, my dungeon shook and the chains fell off'" (p. 24).

REFERENCES

Anosike, Benji, J.O. "Africa and the Afro-American: The Bases for Greater Understanding and Solidarity," JOURNAL OF NEGRO EDUCATION, Volume 51, No. 4.

Aptheker, Herbert. AMERICAN NEGRO SLAVE REVOLTS. New York: Columbia University Press, 1943.

Ashe, Arthur. "Road to Glory." Syndicated Television Program.

Baldwin, James. THE FIRE NEXT TIME. New York: Dell, 1963.

Baldwin, James. NOTES OF A NATIVE SON. New York: Bantam, 1972.

Bauer, Raymond and Alice. "Day to Day Resistance to Slavery." JOURNAL OF NEGRO HISTORY, October, 1942.

Blasingame, John. THE SLAVE COMMUNITY, New York: Oxford University Press, 1972.

Blasingame, John. THE SLAVE COMMUNITY, 1972.

Bryant, Jerry H. "From Death to Life: The Fiction of Ernest Gaines." IOWA REVIEW, 3, (1972), 106-120.

Brown, William Wells. CLOTEL OR THE PRESIDENT'S DAUGHTER. New York: MacMillan Company, 1970.

Clarke, John Henrik, ed. WILLIAM STYRON'S NAT TURNER: TEN BLACK WRITERS RESPOND. Boston: Beacon, 1968.

Cleaver, Eldridge. SOUL ON ICE. New York: Dell, 1968.

Crane, Stephen. THE RED BADGE OF COURAGE. New York: Dell, 1960.

Crane, Stephen. "The Open Boat," Trachtenberg, Alan. AMERICAN LITERATURE, Volume 2, New York: John Wiley, 1978.

Dubois, W.E.B. THE SOULS OF BLACK FOLKS. New York: Fawcett, 1961.

Ellison, Ralph. "Change the Joke and Slip the Yoke" in ADVENTURES OF HUCKLEBERRY FINN. ed. Sculley Bradley, New York: Norton, 1977.

Ellison, Ralph. INVISIBLE MAN. New York: Vintage, 1982.

Farrison, W. Edward. PHYLON PROFILE XVI. "William Wells Brown," PHYLON IX (1948) 13-25.

Farrison, W. Edward. "The Origin of Brown's Clotel," PHYLON XV (1954), 327-347.

Farrison, W. Edward. WILLIAM WELLS BROWN. Chicago: University of Chicago, 1969.

Fetterly, Judy. "Disenchantment: Tom Sawyer in Huckleberry Finn," in ADVENTURES OF HUCKLEBERRY FINN, ed. Sculley, Bradley, New York: Norton, 1977.

Franklin, John Hope. FROM SLAVERY TO FREEDOM, Second ed., New York: Knopf, 1956.

Frazier, R. Franklin. THE NEGRO FAMILY IN THE UNITED STATES. Chicago: University of Chicago Press, 1939.

Gaines, Ernest. THE AUTOBIOGRAPHY OF MISS JANE PITTMAN. New York: Bantam, 1967.

Gossett, Thomas F. UNCLE TOM'S CABIN AND AMERICAN CULTURE, Southern Methodist Press, Dallas, 1985.

Gutman, Herbert G. THE BLACK FAMILY IN SLAVERY AND FREEDOM 1760-1725. New York: Vintage, 1976.

Haley, Alex. ROOTS. New York: Dell, 1977.

Herskovits, Melville J. THE MYTH OF THE NEGRO PAST. Boston: Beacon, 1958.

Hoffman, Daniel G. "Black Magic and White in Huckleberry Finn" in ADVENTURES OF HUCKLEBERRY FINN, ed. Sculley Bradley, New York: Norton, 1977.

Huggins, Nathan J. BLACK ODYSSEY. New York: Vintage, 1979.

Jackson, Edward. BLACK EDUCATION IN CONTEMPORARY AMERICA: A CRISIS IN AMBIGUITY. Wyndam Hall Press, Bristol, IN, 1986.

Jackson, Edward. "Why Black Males Do Not Achieve Academically." Paper read before 13th Annual Conference on The Black Family, March 13, 1986.

Karenga. INTRODUCTION TO BLACK STUDIES. Los Angeles, Kawaida, 1982.

Kelley, William Melvin. A DIFFERENT DRUMMER. Garden City, New York: Anchor, 1962.

Klotman, Phyllis R. "The Passive Resistance in A DIFFERENT DRUMMER, DAY OF ABSENCE and MANY THOUSANDS GONE," SBL 3, iii: 7-12.

Lewis, Richard O. "Literary Conventions in the Novels of William Wells Brown," CLA Volume XXIX, No. 2, Dec., 1985.

Lowery, Joseph. Quoted Sunday Morning CBS News, Jan., 19, 1986.

Marx, Leo. "Mr. Eliot, Mr. Tilling and Huckleberry Finn," ed. Sculley Bradley, New York: Norton, 1977.

Melville, Herman. BILLY BUDD. New York: Signet, 1961.

Miller, Baxter R. "The Etched Flame" of Margaret Walker: Biblical and Literary Recreation in Southern History, TSL, 1981, 26; 157-172.

Nadeau, Robert L. "Black Jesus: A Study of Kelley's A DIFFERENT DRUMMER," SBL, 2 ii: 13-15.

Powell, Charles A. "An Interview with Margaret Walker," Black W, 25, ii, 4-17.

Pryor, Richard. "This Nigger is Crazy," and "Richard Pryor: Live on Sunset Strip," Circa, 1984.

Schuyler, George. BLACK NO MORE. New York: MacMillan, 1971.

Smith, Henry Nash. "A Sound Heart and a Deformed Conscience," in ADVENTURES OF HUCKLEBERRY FINN, ed. Sculley Bradley. New York: Norton, 1977.

Spears, James E. "Black Folk Element in Margaret Walker's JUBILEE," Miss. Fr. Reg., 1980, Spring (14), 13-19, Mississippi Folklore Register.

Stoelting, Winifred L. "Human Dignity and Pride in the Novels of Ernest Gaines," CLAJ, 14: 340-358.

Stowe, Harriet Beecher. UNCLE TOM'S CABIN. New York: Perennial Classics, 1965.

Styron, William. THE CONFESSIONS OF NAT TURNER. New York: Signet, 1968.

Styron, William. "An American Writer," Arts and Entertainment Network, 1985.

Trachtenberg, Alan & Benjamin Mott. AMERICA IN LITERATURE. Vol. 2. New York: John Wiley, 1978.

Twain, Mark. ADVENTURES OF HUCKLEBERRY FINN. ed. Sculley Bradley, New York: Norton, 1977.

Walker, Margaret. HOW I WROTE JUBILEE. New York: Bantam, 1967.

Washington, Booker T. UP FROM SLAVERY. New York: Bantam, 1956.